Dolls of the Art Deco Era
1910 – 1940

Susanna Oroyan

C&T PUBLISHING

© 2004 by Susanna Oroyan

Publisher: Amy Marson

Editorial Director: Gailen Runge

Editors: Sarah Sacks Dunn and Sara Kate MacFarland

Technical Editor: Sara Kate MacFarland

Copyeditor/Proofreader: Stacy Chamness

Cover Designer: Kristy A. Konitzer

Design Director/Book Designer: Kristy A. Konitzer

Illustrator: Tom Oroyan

Production Assistant: Tim Manibusan

Published by C&T Publishing, Inc., P.O. Box 1456,
Lafayette, CA

Title page: *(left)* Doll by Patti Culea, *(center)* doll by Virginia
Robertson, *(right)* doll by elinor peace bailey

Back Cover: *(left)* doll by Drusilla Esslinger, *(bottom right)* doll
by Julie McCullough, *(top right)* doll by Susanna Oroyan;
front and back cover photos by W. Donald Smith

Library of Congress Cataloging-in-Publication Data

Oroyan, Susanna.
    Dolls of the Art Deco era 1910-1940 : collect, restore, create &
play/ Susanna Oroyan.
        p. cm.
    ISBN 1-57120-223-4 (paper trade)
    1. Dolls--Repairing. 2. Dollmaking. 3. Dolls--Collectors and
collecting. 4. Decoration and ornament--Art deco. I. Title.
    TT175.O7599 2003
    745.592'21--dc21

2003011459

Printed in China

10 9 8 7 6 5 4 3 2 1

DEDICATION

This book is dedicated to having fun, and to all of you who help me enjoy dolls and dollmaking more each day.

It isn't possible to name all the names, but these are the people who:

❖ Start doll clubs
❖ Schedule classes in their shops
❖ Put on dollmaking workshops and conferences
❖ Supply and improve our products
❖ Help publish and educate via the media
❖ Share their tips, techniques, and experiences
❖ Take a minute to answer a question or share a source
❖ Show their work so others can be inspired
❖ Stretch their imaginations and abilities
❖ Aren't afraid to try and to fail—more than once
❖ Unreservedly extend the hand and hug of friendship
❖ Remember and support those who are sick or in need of comfort
❖ Say about dollmaking, "That's great!" "I love it!" "Let's do it!"

Betty the Bee's Knees
by Susanna Oroyan
Photo by W. Donald Smith

These are the people who know the process is as important, meaningful, and enjoyable as the product, and who, with serene contentment or great enthusiasm, just love dolls.

These artist friends took time to create their own inventive interpretations of the projects:

Christine Shively, Virginia Robertson, Judi Ward, Patti LaValley, Inez Brasch, Julie McCullough, Patti Culea, Stella Emery, Jean Peeters, Susan Colvin, Dinah Landers, Saralee Hesse, Leilani Lyons, and Patricia Reid.

These collector friends so kindly took time to share photos and research information:

Maralyn Christoffersen, Estelle Johnston, Patricia Brill, Bonnie Grove, Diane Mardis, Frau Wülf, Bergen Fields, and Delores Smith.

Special friend Ginger Burr who got us all involved in playing with bed-dolls.

And my husband, Tom, who makes all the dreams come true.

Table of Contents

Dedication 3

Foreward 7

The Wedding of the Bed-Dolls 8

The Art Deco Doll 14

The Era 20

A Collection, Gallery 24

Collecting 34

Terminology .44

Fabulous Faces, Gallery 48

Amazing Anita, Gallery 52

Wax and wire armature figure Photo by W. Donald Smith

Rosalinde, Gallery 54

The Fashionable French Doll, Gallery 56

South of the Border, Gallery 58

Commédia de l'Arte, Gallery 60

Café Society, Gallery .63

Repairing Your Dolls .64

Repair Stories, Gallery 74

The Smoking Gallery .78

The Zaga of Zona, Gallery 74

The Boarders, Gallery 84

Making Your Own Dolls 88

Vernonia, unmarked Anita-type doll Photo by W. Donald Smith

Designers' Gallery 98

Variations in Cloth, Gallery 101

Project: Basic Bobbi .106

Project: Betty the Bee's Knees 110

Accessories 118

Project: Bed-Doll Dogs 119

Project: Tassel Dolls .123

Sources 126

Index 127

About the Author 128

The Artists 128

Costanza, unmarked American
Stuffed Novelty doll
Photo by W. Donald Smith

Sarah Bernhardt, unmarked
Etta-type doll Photo by W. Donald Smith

Unmarked Blossom-type Photo by W. Donald Smith

Lulu, unmarked W.K.S.-type doll Photo by W. Donald Smith

FOREWARD

I never really played with dolls. Even as a child, I was more interested in making them or finding out how they went together (okay, I was taking them apart!). I made and destroyed any number of dolls for years. Then, I became a serious professional artist. I learned to develop character, work with pose, and create costumes; but my fun came from their design and construction.

One day, all that changed: My friend Ginger introduced her bed-doll crew and their stories at one of our doll-club meetings. She held up Gladys, an authentic 1920s bed-doll, and told the story of Gladys's poor widowed grandmother, who hand-crocheted a dress for Gladys to wear when she went to work in the big city. Ginger talked about Gladys's girlfriends, who insisted she change her name and simple life and who first introduced her to the Moonlight and Roses Ballroom. Then, Ginger held up Rudolpho, a doll of her own design—a slender fellow with slicked-back hair, a pencil-thin moustache, and a come-hither look in his eye. She told us about Gladys and Rudolpho's tempestuous romance. When Ginger produced a baby she had made using a vintage doll face mask, she informed us (in a hushed tone) that Gladys's baby, Barbara, "has Rudolpho's chin!" (See page 8 for the whole story.)

Since that day, I've never looked back—I had to have a bed-doll so I could play, too. From then on, it became a passion. My friends and I buy, make, and gossip for and about our dolls. We have had a wedding, tea parties, and luncheons; we have a multitude of stories about their escapades. In my house, some have come, some have gone, but as I write almost two dozen countesses, coeds, starlets, and more live under my bed, having cocktail parties, cat fights, and costume fittings—and even going to movie premiers—while I sleep.

Affordable for collectors, accessible for makers, these ladies provide hours and hours of pure, imaginative fun. Come join me in their magical, mystical world.

The Wedding
of the Bed-Dolls

Photos by W. Donald Smith

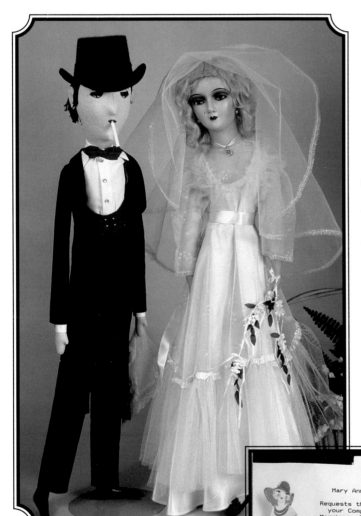

One of the all-time best doll parties was our friend Ginger Burr's wedding of bed-dolls Jackie and Rudolpho. We and our dolls received invitations, everyone dressed in classy duds, we feasted on cake and ice cream, and Ginger presented her bed-dolls with the story told on these pages.

Gladys, one of Rudolpho's romantic conquests, is shown here with her baby, *Barbara* (who has her daddy's chin). Gladys got this new lacy dress to go with her friends to the Moonlight and Roses Ballroom (a place she and Rudolpho used to frequent). Gladys is an Anita doll; Ginger designed and made the baby with a vintage mask face.

Rudolpho left poor Gladys and Barbara, then had a brief fling with *Flossie* (he called her his little "Frou-Frou") in Paris, where this photo of her was taken. However, he couldn't resist his old haunts: He turned up again at the Moonlight and Roses Ballroom, where he met Jackie.

Rudolpho, the groom, is a cloth doll Ginger designed and created. You'll soon see what a scoundrel he can be.

Here are **Jackie,** the bride; her mother, **Mary Ann Toinette;** and her sister, **Geraldine,** waiting for the wedding to begin. (All three are common bed-dolls that have been restored and redressed.) Needless to say, Mother was not pleased with Jackie's choice of Rudolpho, which accounts for her sour look; in fact, if you look closely, you can see the name "Bob" on her bonnet ribbons. She relented, pursed her mouth, and determined to make the best of it by inviting all the bed-dolls in town to the wedding.

Bed-dolls have many friends, including novelty dolls. **Maria the Maid** and **Dr. Ripon** are souvenir dolls imported from Mexico.

Jackie's husband, **"Cowboy" Bob,** is a "put-together" figure made from a 1940s novelty head and a body built by Ginger. He mysteriously disappeared on their wedding day—just a little more than seven years ago. Jackie was now officially a widow, and Rudolpho was in need of a reason not to get deported. Marriage was proposed.

Madame Rozella, the Gypsy fortuneteller, warned the dolls about making too much whoopee. Madame Rozella should know: She has two left hands, and that gives her special "powers." It is not uncommon to find a doll with two of the same hands—manufacturers were not all that careful.

Paying no heed to the warning, the wedding began. Just as the wedding party stood at the altar, however, a voice from the back of the church cried, "Those wedding bells shall not ring out!" Everyone turned to see Bob, Jackie's long-lost husband, clutching their wedding certificate. Bob declared himself the victim of an accident. Right after he and Jackie were married, he said, he went to get the car; in the parking lot, he was hit and knocked head-over-heels into a truck headed for Mexico. (Poor Geraldine, as you can see, was devastated that she wouldn't get to be the bridesmaid.)

Once in Mexico, Bob found himself with a case of amnesia. Coincidentally, Dr. Ripon, an old friend of the family, was the doctor treating Bob in Mexico. It took Dr. Ripon all seven years of his disappearance to restore his memory. During Bob's treatment, the doctor's daughter, beautiful *Lolita,* fell in love with him. You can see how she took the news when she heard he remembered he had a wife.

Lolita met **Cuthbert** at the wedding, saw immediately that he was a much better-looking fellow, and accordingly set her sights on him.

All's well that ends well. Lolita and Cuthbert are still together. Mary Ann Toinette was extremely pleased to see Jackie and Bob reunited. Dr. Ripon took up plastic surgery and now does regular work for the Hollywood crowd. Gladys gave up Saturday nights at the ballroom, took courses in business management, and ended up the owner of a very successful real-estate company. Baby Barbara graduated from Harvard with a graduate degree in political science and is currently on the White House executive staff. Geraldine joined the army to see the world. Jackie and Bob are living happily ever after and are now on the road in their motor home, visiting grandchildren around the country. Poor Rudolpho was so humiliated that he quietly left the wedding during all the confusion and hasn't been heard from since. As for Madame Rozella's predictions…well, everyone thinks she was just talking through her turban.

If you want to join the party and make a little whoopee with your dolls, there are plenty out in the world waiting for you to make, collect, rejuvenate, and tell stories about. Party on!

The Art Deco Doll

See page 44 for a list of doll-specific terminology used throughout the book.

Art figure? No, the Lilli Baitz design forms the framework for a dresser lamp. Photo by Pat Brill

Although many people think of dolls as play-things for children, dolls have a long history of being used for and by adults. From the Renaissance onward, dolls were sent around the courts of Europe—and even overseas—dressed in "current" fashions. Mechanical dolls amused and delighted adults, and many grown-ups crafted detailed dollhouses and elaborate crèche scenes to impress their guests. Dolls populated historical dioramas in museums and galleries. Older girls and ladies purchased very fine "companion" dolls. The ladies would show off their sewing prowess by making delicately sewn wardrobes for the dolls.

Between 1890 and the beginning of World War I, the art-doll prominently displayed both characters and costumes. Characters from Balzac's *Comédie Humaine* were made by Madame Marter, while other designers made dolls that imitated great actresses of the period. Some fashion houses made art-doll figures as gifts for their customers—the dolls showed off their trendy styles.

This cloth-body doll has a composition breastplate, head, and arms, and was probably made in the early 1920s. Notice its open dome and glass eyes. These features show how the industry was in transition between nineteenth-century techniques and the "modern" dolls of the Art Deco era.
Photo by Maralyn Christoffersen

These cloth mask faces were made to be purchased and completed as dolls by the home craftsmen. The manufacturer's name, Gluckin & Co., New York is printed at the side of the neck. Photos by W. Donald Smith

The fashion house Paul Poiret, for example, gave away figures dressed in exact replicas of customers' new ensembles. Dolls from the *Lafitte Desirat* collection are considered to be the most elegant.

Some of these little fashion dolls were meant to be carried around—a form of advertising. This trend began to spread as it was shown in *Erté's* elegant illustrations in *Harper's Bazaar* magazine. Shortly before World War I, lady dolls also appeared in the unusual form of night-dress cases—or what we now call a pajama bag. Better versions, made in England by firms like Dean's and Chad Valley, had silk faces and satin dresses. None of these art-dolls were made in great quantity or sold in masses, but they did set the scene for the incredible art and bed-doll fad of the 1920s.

After World War I, the design style now known as Art Deco began to emerge. A mix of styles from the 1920s and 1930s, the Art Deco "era" is generally thought of as from the 1910s through the 1940s, with the stereotypical period usually referred to as the 1920s. Following World War I, dolls changed along with society. Elegant art-dolls—purely for show—were made in the 1920s by companies like *Les Poupees Gerb's* in Paris. An amazing array of dolls by Lenci also began to stream out of Italy. Lenci's lady dolls, characters and clowns were made of felt pressed in steel molds. The art figures often featured thematic treatments of the exotic, foreign, fantastic, or mythological. Our modern artist dolls are a direct continuation of this type.

World War I and the Movies

The European art-doll phenomenon could well have been the result of World War I. The effect of four years of war in Western Europe was devastating. The war redrew the map of Europe and destroyed social and economic traditions. Youthful survivors found no "grown-up" established world of custom to fit back into, so they continued to be the children they were before the war. With lost illusions and "don't give a damn" attitudes, they drove their cars fast, drank and partied, embraced modern abstract art and literature…and played with dolls.

In the United States, prior to World War I, entertainment for much of the country consisted of traveling lecturers and theatrical companies, mostly of the vaudeville variety. In the larger urban areas there were permanent theaters, but far more common entertainment took place in church basements and school

Irma Naroditskya's modern version of a silent movie star doll portrays beautifully what many of the period dolls showed: glamour, coyness, and a hint of mystery. Photo by Jerry Anthony

gymnasiums. By 1920, movies, rapidly developed in the World War I years, were here to stay. Every one-horse town had a movie theater. Cities had movie palaces even before movies talked. Movies were accessible: You didn't have to dress up, and they only cost a dime or two. Anyone could go and everyone did. Hollywood musicals offered the hope of better times and a temporary escape from daily troubles.

Before World War I, female role models were the ladies of high society. Stage actresses had always been considered "loose" and not to be taken as proper role models. After the war, titles were not worth much, and high society was composed of "new money." Movie people became trendsetters in a new, jazzier age. Their hairstyles, lifestyles, and clothing were there to be copied. Movie magazines and ladies' home-arts publications abounded for ideas and patterns. Anyone could make a doll to imitate that life—and it seems almost everyone did. More than anything, the bed-doll, boudoir doll, flapper doll, and mascot doll fad of the 1920s was grown-ups playing dolls—and may be the only time when all society played dolls.

The Dolls

Art-doll, boudoir doll, bed-doll . . . when I got interested in the period, I thought I knew what they were: the long-limbed ladies with the big skirts made in the 1920s. (Not exactly.) The more I learned, the more I found there were all kinds. If you want to collect them, it's good to know how they are classified. If you want to make them, you will want to try all the types. And, of course, the more you know about their life and times, the better you can play. Here's a little background to get you started.

When we talk about the dolls of the 1920s, we find that almost any doll not obviously and specifically made only for child's play was called an "art" or "novelty" doll. Nowadays, we think of an "art-doll" as something created by an individual studio artist, a one-of-a-kind or a member of a small handmade edition. The art-dolls of the 1920s were also called bed-dolls, boudoir dolls, French dolls, sofa dolls, pillow dolls, mascots, wobblies, flappers, smokers, and many other names.

While it would be nice to find one or two characteristics, such as looks or material to separate them from other dolls, they were made from the usual doll materials of their era—cloth, composition, and wax. While many were made to represent females, just as many were clowns, characters, and ethnic types. Most popular was the eighteenth-century Marie Antoinette and the romantic styles of the 1840s, followed by the Pierrot, Pierette, Harlequin, and *Commédia* figures from 18th century Italian theater.

Nowadays, the term "bed-doll" seems to refer to the low-grade, mass-produced models. That term is probably better applied to dolls specifically costumed in large, full skirts that could be spread prettily on the bed or sofa. The majority of the dolls that still are around today are these full-skirted, long-limbed ladies.

A typical **W-K-S Bed-Doll**, with long limbs, sidecast eyes, and a full, fancy skirt that lets just the tip of her shoe peek out.
Photo by Pat Brill

Then there is the Flapper doll. Vamp, tramp, scamp—the flapper doll was the elemental form of the decade. This doll, usually made with a soft, stuffed cotton body in a very elongated flat-chested form, with a cloth or composition face, sitting casually, painted in the flirty "vamp" style, was the one type unique to its era. These dolls truly did represent their contemporary world. They often came undressed, with their arms tied around their folded-up legs. They had bobbed hair-dos, smoked cigarettes, and, when dressed, wore the sporty, sleek, and slinky fashions of the day. They were often made with faces resembling movie stars. While the elegant art-doll generally remained a European production, the flapper doll was made-in-America fashion. These were the bee's knees! (See page 106 for instructions and patterns for making your own version.)

Today, when we differentiate dolls-for-adults from the 1920s, we do it as follows: *Art-dolls* are usually by named designers like Lenci, Wellings, and Steiff. They usually have very well-made bodies and costumes, and they aren't always long-legged. *Boudoir* dolls are almost always long-limbed and have nicely done costumes and highly colored composition or silk faces. *Bed-dolls* are long-limbed, composition or plain cloth, costumed in more simple designs, and not so well made. All the rest are considered "novelty" dolls.

Note: Americans tend to use the term bed-doll rather than boudoir doll as a generic name—it is an easier word to say for an English speaker. In this book, we will use the generic term bed-doll to indicate a mass-produced, long-limbed lady doll.

The Era

When we think of the 1920s, we think of fast cars, Romeos and racy ladies, short skirts and braless tops, cigarettes, bathtub gin, speakeasies, and jazz dancing. Truth is, that was only some of it—really, very little of it. Images of any era are always remembered in the extreme, usually the extremes of the youth of that time. The real story is much more sedate and mundane.

The pleasures and leisure of the 1920s were really simple community and family-oriented affairs. Married women were not expected to work outside the home. Typically, a middle-class-married couple lived in town, in a rented house— a mansion by today's standards. Homes at the turn of the century commonly were two stories with large rooms. New homes, built "bungalow" style, were much smaller. The magazine version of the 1920s backyard had a vegetable garden, a formal garden, and a separate play area for the children. The garage was tucked far to the back of the property and was just large enough to hold the family car, the push lawn mower, and basic handheld garden tools. A hired gardener, who would bring his own equipment, would do the heavier garden work.

If you're longing for a home from the 1920s, first take into consideration its likely features. It had four bedrooms to accommodate a family, but only one bathroom. The storage was miniscule by today's standards. The good-sized dining room also functioned as the family room, was a place for homework, and housed mother's and father's "easy" chairs for doing hand sewing and reading the newspaper in the evenings.

Imagine working in the "modern" kitchen. There was a singular lack of counter and cupboard space. The room was just large enough to hold a freestanding sink, a free-standing range, and one "Hoosier," or combination china-baking-storage and countertop cupboard. Refrigerator? Maybe. More likely, there was an icebox located just inside the back door where the iceman could bring in his drippy block once a week. Utility room? Well, that was a fold-down ironing board in the kitchen. The laundry was, of course, in the basement or cellar.

Typically, very few people owned an automobile. They walked within their small town or neighborhood, and took a trolley or train for longer trips. The husband worked five or six days a week, while the wife stayed home and took care of the house. In the country, life differed only in that the automobile came sooner and the wife usually gardened, canned, ran the chicken house and the dairy, and did larger amounts of cooking for farm hands.

A good housewife followed the "days of the week" schedule. Monday: washing day; Tuesday: ironing day; Wednesday: baking day; Thursday: sewing day; Friday: cleaning day; Saturday: shopping day; and Sunday was the day of rest. They even embroidered dishtowels with motifs to remind them of this schedule. Few ladies had hired help, but as this was the "modern era;" they did have washing machines, electric irons, and vacuum cleaners. If she was efficient, a lady could almost always complete her daily chores before noon.

Here's a typical Monday: Our lady of the house would get up early and cook a breakfast of eggs, bacon, and hot oatmeal. After making lunches, making the beds, and sending her children off to school, she would sort the wash, separating it into "whites," "colors," "darks," and "dainties." Whites and colors—usually coarse woven cotton or linen—were washed with bleach and run through a hot rinse and then a cool rinse with bluing, then starched with dry starch mixed with boiling water. Each batch had to be run by hand through the wringer of the washing machine (or in some cases hand-wrung) into large laundry tubs. The end result was several baskets full of heavy wet clothes that had to be carried outside and hung out to dry—in order. Underwear usually went on the inside lines—or even inside the sheets—because you wouldn't want the neighbors to see the unmention-

ables. Socks hung two to a peg. There was an art to sliding the clothespin basket down the line, pinning an item, holding its loose end, and picking up the next out of the basket in a smooth, economical movement. After the laundry was hung, our lady might hand-wash her dainties—silk undies and woolies. With luck, she finished in time to change out of her work smock and into a housedress covered with a nice apron for the afternoon. (No lady wore trousers!)

During the afternoon, while the laundry dried, there might be time for some embroidery or to read ladies' magazines. Then all the laundry had to be taken down, some folded and put away, and some set aside to be dampened for the next day's ironing. Few steam irons and no drip-dry meant starched items had to be damp to press smooth. About 4:00 p.m. she would begin supper, preparing a plain meat and potatoes main course (maybe with cheese and sausage on the side), a boiled vegetable, possibly some canned fruit, rarely a salad, always bread and butter, and always a dessert. Then, she would wash up and spend the evening reading, doing handwork, or visiting until an early bedtime.

No television. No radio. No outside job.

Not all days were like Monday. Some days had a little more time, but this time was usually taken up with sewing and household decorating projects. Ladies did get together in the afternoons to play cards, visit, or do church or organizational work. At home or out, ladies always had some handwork project in progress. A housewife was judged by the state of her linens and her ability with a needle. There were towels to be monogrammed, napkins to be hemmed and embroidered, doilies and tablecloths to crochet, sweaters and mittens to knit, children's clothes and curtains to be made.

Social life consisted of visiting regularly with neighbors over the fence or over coffee and playing cards in the evening. People went to church or lodge groups perhaps once a week, and almost everyone went to church at least once on Sunday. The very popular movie houses changed bills twice a week and many put on weekday specials. Only toward the end of the 1920s, when radios became common, did people begin to stay at home more.

A very different life than our picture of the "Roaring Twenties." Did they, indeed "roar?"

Yes, in the movies, in magazines, in Hollywood, and in the "fast" societies of New York, London, Paris, and Berlin. Other people did, in other places. Rich people, movie people. What trickled down to the public in magazines and movies was the image of the mad, gay, expensive life that a few other people lived. But what a fun image it was. Everyone wanted to try—even just a little bit. New cars, bobbed hair, shorter skirts, and the image of the vamp—the bed-doll face—were how ordinary people could participate.

The Fad Begins

While the art-doll concept was certainly not new in the 1920s, it exploded in popularity during that time. To understand why, remember that the 1920s and 1930s were the era of frivolous flappers and monumental movies. The flourishes of Art Nouveau and the opulence of the Victorian era were a thing of the past, and the Art Deco period brought in its emphasis on all things sleek, shiny, and, most importantly, modern.

Dolls, like their people owners, always reflect the design milieu of their era. The fussy, child-like, often unreal-looking dolls of the nineteenth century represented the rather stifled role of women and children in society. After World War I, women got the vote, bobbed their hair, raised their hemlines, and went to work. Dolls did too. As dolls changed, they became a fad: Every house had to have one or more. Once that fad hit the movie-mad United States in the mid-1920s, demand increased even more, and production really took off.

The Widow Weed is a very lovely lady who just might be contemplating opening a restaurant in Hollywood—maybe in the shape of a derby hat!—after all, a girl can be a business lady in these modern days. Photo by W. Donald Smith

A Collection

Here, for your viewing pleasure, are several pages of lovelies. Most of these are in quite good condition; many have been lovingly and carefully restored. Browse and enjoy!

The ultimate couple! Made to look like actor Clark Gable and one of his lovely leading ladies, these two Blossom Company figures represent the great infatuation with movie stars in the 1930s. Clark's face appears to be oil-painted, while hers is painted cloth—and has the trademark Blossom eyelashes. Photo by Bonnie Groves

A true flapper bride, with her dashing (if slightly foppish) groom. She requested a new dress for the ceremony, but her owner also carefully preserved the original one intact under the new creation. Photo by W. Donald Smith

This piece is more figure than doll, yet she is a doll. She is made of painted composition parts assembled on a wire armature framework. Her costume and hair are of vintage manufacture, although the dress appears to be homemade. Photo by W. Donald Smith

Not all dolls of the 1920s were long-limbed. This Majorette, a German-made doll with a flocked composition head, is about 20" tall. The German-made dolls always seem to have very delicately rendered eye highlights. Photo by W. Donald Smith

Art-dolls of the 1920s were frequently referred to as French dolls, probably because of their very stylish and well-made costumes. This doll has a molded head covered with silk hair and a cloth body with painted plaster arms and legs. Her dress was—and still is—in mint condition. Photo by W. Donald Smith

A very special half-doll made up as a pincushion—her shattered silk skirts hide many vintage pins underneath. Half-dolls in original costume, with arms away from the body, holding an item, or with a hat like this one are the most-desired dolls of serious collectors. Photo by W. Donald Smith

This Roaring Twenties flapper is called **Madge Smith** or just "that Smith girl" by her owner. She has cellophane neck trim; most likely she was a Cubeb smoker, meant to be mounted on a stick. These detailed, trimmed heads were sometimes called cheer sticks or rally sticks. Photo by W. Donald Smith

We call her **Wilma**; she's a later W-K-S type with a short, busty body, still in her original dress. The later bed-dolls dolls were definitely made to have full-circle skirts to spread out over a pillow. Her hat and the gold bodice trim, made of vintage materials, were added. Photo by W. Donald Smith

Another interesting molded silk-face doll. We call her **Maria Espadrilla** just because she has a rather Spanish look.

Photo by W. Donald Smith

This beauty is in mint condition and is an excellent example of the silk mask face with an elaborate hairstyle. She has a hangtag that says *"Printemps."* A Paris department store of that name is known to have had a doll workshop in 1918. Very possibly she—and others like her—is one of their products. Her owner called her **Blanche** and dressed her using a 1920s McCall's doll dress pattern. Reprints of the old doll dress patterns can be found on many Internet doll sites. Photo by W. Donald Smith

Ivy Fern Greenleaf, the Acrobatic Dancer, was built from a kit face and dressed as a clown by her present owner. It is not unusual to find bed-dolls with really outrageous hair colors. Ivy's green embroidery floss coiffure came already attached to the kit head. Photo by W. Donald Smith

We think *Costanza* (or *"Connie"* as we know her) is a movie studio secretary who dresses up in a costume to suggest a Polish background. She looks very much like a clown doll advertised by the Unique Novelty Doll Company, but she has no marks. Photo by W. Donald Smith

The Divine Sarah Bernhardt is a lovely molded-face doll who arrived with only her original shoes. Her owner dressed her using one of the vintage McCall's patterns. Although she is unmarked, she looks very much like an Etta doll. Photo by W. Donald Smith

Sonja—shown here with her dog, *Boris*—is a cloth-faced doll that has had a new dress of old materials made for her. Notice how the four cloth faces on this page all vary in their shapes. Photo by W. Donald Smith

The lounging suit hides this Anita doll's original Buster Brown chest label. She has wonderful high-color facial painting. (See detail on page 34) Photo by W. Donald Smith

The Estelle Taylor Love Doll: That's what it says on her tag. You figure it out—or just enjoy her sweet puckered mouth and her pompoms. Photo by W. Donald Smith

This breathtaking 20" all-original French doll appears to be receiving the gallant attention of a wonderful French gentleman. A second look, however, tells us that he is really wearing the cassock and beret of a priest. He isn't really a bed-doll, but perhaps the girls could use his spiritual guidance. Photo by Bergen Fields

Marguerite came to her owner in this dreadful state. She has much more blocky features and form than most bed-dolls, but her braided hair is carefully coiled. Photo by W. Donald Smith

Since this photo was taken, the owner gave *Auntie Olivia* a new hat. She is a big girl—about 30" tall. Her stuffed figure was sewn from a printed fabric panel. First noticed by the doll collectors in the 1950s, we really don't know when these dolls were manufactured, but they just scream to be included with any bed-doll collection. Photo by W. Donald Smith

This is a very nice example of the Anita-type doll. We have to say "type" because she is unmarked and has a slightly broader face than the typical marked Anita. Her owner has dressed her in richly embroidered vintage fabric. Photo by W. Donald Smith

Called *Norma Desmond* by her owner, this gal has taken to carrying around the bottle (usually tastefully disguised in a brown paper bag). Her friends call her "Wild Turkey." She is what is called a "high-color" composition. Photo by W. Donald Smith

One of the prize collectible dolls from the early Art Deco years was the beautiful C&O Dressel flapper doll, shown here in newly made lingerie, as well as a smashing orange jumpsuit with jacket. She is about 14" tall and has an articulated composition body. The head is porcelain with sleep eyes.

Photos by W. Donald Smith

This smoker has a papier-mâché head with a stuffed velvet body. Her large hat is held in place with a vintage hatpin. Photo by W. Donald Smith

Many dolls were made to portray clowns. **Dots** has been dressed in clown mode and set up with a curly-haired dog to help in her act. Photo by W. Donald Smith

Here's a very pretty girl with an especially nice hairdo. Her owner dressed her with an Austrian folk costume apron. As usual, there are no markings but, as her torso extends almost to the waist, she is probably a Sterling. Photo by W. Donald Smith

This figure appears to be an Anita smoker. The costume is vintage black velvet with gold lace trim. Photo by W. Donald Smith

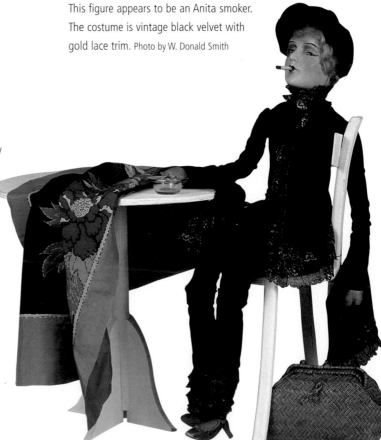

Solid or wax-covered composition dolls are rare. When you find them, they are usually small; but this one is 29" tall. Her hands are posed in a very coquettish gesture, as if she is beckoning to the recipient of her sidelong glance. Photo by Pat Brill

Zizi looks as if she is ready for some fun. Her printed cloth face shows the extreme end of the Art Deco makeup style. Her diminutive companion is a Norah Wellings sailor; he has a mask face and stuffed body. Wellings sailors were typically sold as souvenirs on steamships—this yeoman came from the ocean liner *Empress of Britain.* Photo by W. Donald Smith

Collecting

As you can see, this doll, made by the Anita Novelty Company, was made to advertise shoes. Photo by W. Donald Smith

A rare and unusual all-original Cubeb harem smoker that may be a prototype. The doll has pierced garnet earrings and a molded metal bangle bracelet. Photo by Pat Brill

Those of us who play the bed-doll game often feel like orphans in the collector world. We buy them, restore and repair them, and love them; but we don't have very much hard information about them. Rarely were any marked, and few of these have survived. Since most were found in dreadful state and many were cheap novelty dolls, not many collectors really cared about researching their origins. For years, we have had to love them for who they are, not who made them. And that wasn't hard to do.

However, in recent years collectors have been finding each other. Little by little, information is coming together, and pieces are being fit into the puzzle. Some collectors have dolls with an original mark or tag. Others provide copies of vintage catalogs or advertisements that show the doll and the manufacturer's name together. Even as shared information increases, there is still a long way to go. I hope that by sharing the following information with you, I also further the knowledge of all collectors and provide more opportunities for new information to trickle into the doll community.

A doll's manufacturer is sometimes more difficult to determine than the doll's purpose. Many, like the Cubeb smokers and the Buster Brown doll, were made to advertise other products. Some were made for department stores, and have tags such as *Printemps* in Paris or Macy's in New York. It also appears that some of the more elaborately costumed dolls were made by home craftsmen and sold at bazaars featuring ethnic art in the early 1920s. These dolls were not themselves permanently marked. However, many collectors believe that most dolls had stickers, hangtags, or marked boxes. These identifying items were taken off and lost when the doll was originally bought and displayed. If you find a doll with its original box or label, you have found a special treasure.

Even if a doll has no identifying mark, there are some clues to identify its age. Generally, the impression is that in the 1920s and 1930s craftsmanship was slightly better, perhaps because the dolls were so popular at that time and they were being purchased as home décor. The later dolls were often made as carnival prizes and souvenirs—cheap throwaway novelties rather than decorative art, and therefore not worth the time and effort to manufacture well.

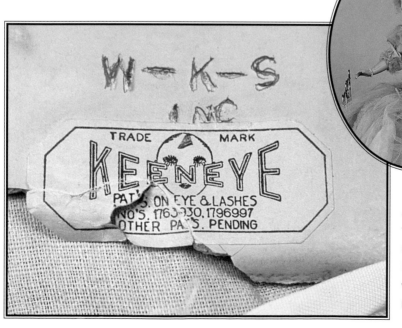

In the 1950s the bed-doll fashion continued, in modified form. Some were simply fancy dresses on commercial dolly bodies. This one, however, looks like an older mold was used.
Photo by W. Donald Smith

All serious collectors are very concerned with finding manufacturer's marks on a doll. Bed-dolls; however, were very rarely marked. This Keeneye tag with incised W-K-S marks would be very unusual to find.
Photo by W. Donald Smith

The Doll Makers

The jolly clown *(left)* and the very pretty girl *(below)* are pressed mask-face felt dolls made in the 1920s by the Lenci Company in Italy. These dolls with their sharply painted features and well-made jointed bodies, including separate fingers, are considered to be extremely desirable. A collector could expect to pay a very substantial amount for a Lenci figure in good condition. Photo by W. Donald Smith

This is a doll marked W-K- and we think it should be W-K-S. The type is very common to the 1930s and 1940s. They were often dressed in satin and lace costumes with very full skirts and large matching hats. Don't be surprised if there is no hair under the hat—most came with only as much hair as would show. This doll type is usually referred to as "common" or "composition and cloth." They are the ones you are most likely to find. Photo by W. Donald Smith

$\mathcal{C}$ompanies that made novelty dolls often marked or tagged their work, but production, though well done, must not have been large; very few clearly-marked dolls turn up these days. In addition, unmarked boudoir dolls made by small family or artisan groups were plentiful in Europe after World War I. Identifying these dolls is therefore sometimes dicey. Then, like now, manufacturers were in the business to sell units of product. The idea was to be fast and economical, and to make the wholesale buyer happy with a quick response. The following manufacturers are most well known to doll collectors.

The Anita Novelty Company: Affiliated with the European Doll Manufacturing Company in 1929. Volume 2 of *Coleman's Encyclopedia of Dolls* states that H. Altbuck, who claimed to have invented the French doll, was a member of this company. There are many versions of the composition Anita head—flange heads, shoulder plate heads, smokers, and ones with heads that turned. The Anita Company also appears to have made dolls for other companies' promotions, such as Buster Brown shoes. Earlier dolls had high color and had very vampy-looking faces.

Blossom: This manufacturer made dolls with cloth heads and very distinctive eyelashes; they were often very elegantly dressed.

Bloom: The typical example is cloth with very elongated eyes and a pointy-pouty mouth. Its body is marked with a stamp.

Chad Valley: Primarily known for soft toy dolls, this 1920s company made bed-dolls in both Pierrot characters and flapper girls.

Etta, Inc.: Miss Etta Kidd founded this company with all female workers. They made clowns, which sometimes incorporated voices or hand-painted cloth. They also made cowboys, pirates, adults, pillows, novelty bags, and long-limbed ladies in romantic outfits. They sold their doll's clothing and shoes separately.

European Doll Manufacturing Company (EDMA): After 1929, EDMA merged with the Anita Novelty Company. Emphasis was on the production of boudoir dolls, French dolls, and flapper types, but they also made pillows, bags, and other novelties using the heads.

French Dollmakers/Gre Poir. 1927-30 Manufactured "specialty" dolls with molded heads made of felt. The dolls usually had mohair wigs and cloth bodies, jointed at the neck, shoulders, and sometimes hips. Costuming and workmanship in examples show quality production. Thumbs were separated from hands with fingers indicated by stitching. Eugenie Poir is said to have been the designer. Gre Poir became part of the French Dollmakers company. The doll shown here has a sewn-in cloth label that reads, "The French Dollmakers/ Vanda/ My hair can be washed/ I can be dry cleaned." Other company tags indicated they could be cleaned with art gum.

Gerling: This company manufactured *Hotsy Totsy* and *Black Bottom* dolls from 1926 to 1927; they switched to *Whoopee* and *Dancing Dolls* in 1928.

Jane Gray Company: They specialized in cloth dolls, including the *Kuddles,* and designed the *Black Bottom* doll produced by Gerling.

Holzer et cie **(Brazil):** This company made felt dolls, often dressed in costumes with felt embellishments. They were usually tagged or labeled "Brazil" or "Made in Brazil."

Les Poupees Gerb's: These dolls were cloth-covered, with molded faces, very fine facial rendering, and exquisitely detailed costumes.

Mutual Novelty Company: These dolls were cigarette girls with composition heads, bobbed hair, trouser suits with belts, and vertically striped fabric on the pockets and cuffs. They were very similar to Lenci Fadettes. These dolls are generally referred to as *Cubebs* (after a type of cigarette, which contained a spice ingredient to sooth the throat).

Lafitte, Desirat: While not boudoir dolls, these 12" dolls are very much their precursors. They are truly art-dolls, made to show French fashions in the years 1900 to 1919. Their bodies were wrapped wire armatures; their heads and hands were wax. Clothing—including shoes, hats, and gloves—was extremely realistically rendered. A fine, representative group of these dolls is in the permanent collection of the *Musée des Arts Decoratifs* in Paris.

Lenci Company: Founded by the artist Elena Scaveni in Italy, Lenci (a nickname for Elena) dolls are among art-dolls most sought after by collectors. Lenci was early and prolific in producing several lines of felt dolls: six-inch *mascottes,* jointed ladies, *commédia* figures, and numerous character types. Lenci dolls were made by steam pressing felt in steel molds. All were marked on the bottom of the foot.

Standard Doll Company: Affiliated with Keeneye, this company made several types of bed-dolls.

Sterling Doll Company: This company made boudoir dolls beginning in 1930. The dolls are noted for the company mark on the torso, as well as a full torso that extends below the bust nearly to the waist. Their arms were strung into their bodies, and some had inset eyelashes. They also made cloth dolls.

T.A.F. (*Talleres de Arte Fuste*-Spain): A 1934 catalog shows very elaborately costumed 32" boudoir dolls made by this company.

Unique Novelty Company: Boudoir dolls and pajama-bag dolls were made there.

Wellings: In 1926 Norah Wellings, who had been a designer for Chad Valley Toy Company, opened a doll factory with her brother, Leonard. Wellings dolls are cloth, notably soft types such as velvet, velveteen, and plush. The heads are molded, and most have side-glancing eyes and painted features. Wellings produced a 36" bed-doll of the "pretty lady" variety with a bland, more realistic, smiling face. The company also produced novelty dolls of velveteen dressed as sailors, which were sold as souvenirs on steamship lines. They also made black, ethnic, and Hawaiian or tropical costumed dolls often found in bed-doll collections. Wellings dolls were marked with sewn-in tags.

W.K.S. and Keeneye: The Keeneye trademark was registered in 1931 on a Victor Keney design. This trademark is sometimes found on dolls marked with an incised W-K, but other dolls are marked W-K-S. (Possibly the S in the stamp did not always impress; or, the S may have stood for Standard.) The earlier dolls had almost heart-shaped faces; inset eyelashes, composition shoulder, head, and limbs; and molded-on shoes. They also strongly resemble dolls referred to by collectors as Sterling. Later dolls marked Keeneye seem to have larger heads, more coarse features, and more "blobby" lips. Some later dolls have inset eyelashes. Most of these dolls have the shorter, more realistically proportioned cloth body.

Becoming a Collector

Are you hooked yet?

Ready to collect and play? If so, you may be lucky enough to get a doll as a gift, but most collectors have to brave the marketplace. While shopping for bed-dolls can be one of the best playtime experiences a doll collector can have, it does require that you first learn about what you should look for.

Before you go shopping, decide what you want. Do you want to purchase a doll you can play with? Will you be looking for a mint-condition doll to display? Or do you simply want to use your sewing and craft skills to rescue, repair, and restore otherwise unwanted dolls?

If you decide you want an authentic bed-doll, you can probably find one by going to a doll show or looking for dealers and auctions on the Internet. Keep your eyes open just about anywhere else: junk stores, thrift shops, antique shows, doll sales, yard sales, and maybe even your great-aunt's attic.

Very few original dolls that you find for sale today will bear the manufacturer's mark. Of the more than fifty original bed-dolls I photographed for this book, only three were marked. Fortunately, most collectors don't focus on proof of pedigree; quality, condition, and character matter more. Your eye and your personal taste—and, of course, your pocketbook—will have to be your guide. If you're interested in a doll for the doll's sake, his or her lineage won't be as important to you as whether you like the way the doll looks, or the potential you see within it.

Esmé, a unique, early wax art doll. The poured wax head, torso, and limbs are assembled on a wire and cork armature. Her owner has dressed her in vintage fabrics. Photo by W. Donald Smith

Collectors, though, want to treat the doll as a historical artifact true to its original period. In order to do that well, we have to know what the object looked like when it was new or in use. When you see a doll marked "excellent" or "very good condition," you'll know that the doll is the way it always was; it hasn't been altered. (This is also the reason why when we restore or repair, we want to be careful to "put it the way it was" rather than to "make it over.")

WHAT SHOULD YOU PAY?

Price always works as a function of demand. The finest dolls of any type will always be most desirable and, correspondingly, their prices tend to rise over the years. This seems to be what has happened with the bed-dolls over the last ten years. The better and more unusual types have increased in price, while the cost of the more common varieties has stayed fairly stable. This means that there can be a big gap between the highest price for a common type and the lowest price for an unusual type.

Generally, though, the value of any object is what someone is willing to pay for it. A serious collector will pay more for a doll that is closer to the original state, while collectors who like to have fun "fixing-up" will not expect to pay much. That means, to a certain extent, you and other buyers can decide the price. If a seller has a doll priced at $100 and six people want it but refuse to pay that amount, simple economics should tell the seller that either he is in the wrong marketplace or his price is too high.

A true market price is one that reflects what several different people at all ends of the country actually paid for similar items. Price guides are usually based on that information. If a certain type of doll sells for $1,000 on the East Coast, $900 in Los Angeles, and $750 in Kansas; then market price or asking price in a price guide will appear as a range between $750 and $1,000.

This all-original Anita-type harem girl has lovely facial detail. Her costume is faded and the lace is a little tattered, but she is in lovely shape. Expect her asking price to be at the high end in any price guide. Photos by Pat Brill

Price ranges also depend a great deal on condition. Generally, prices in guides reflect prices for dolls in good, better, or excellent condition. Still, at the low end of any range the doll should be clean, not cracked, with original hair, in repairable condition. Maybe the costume is uninteresting and fairly worn or poorly chosen, but low end of the range still means the doll is in basically good condition.

When should the price be lower than the low-end listings? Broken, dirty, or incomplete dolls always should be less than the range in the guide. Badly cracked composition; soiled, water-spotted, or mildewed fabrics; missing parts, clothing, or wigs: These are the dolls that will require major work in restoration and costuming. Even if a restorer did an excellent job, the repairs would show and the doll would not be anything like the original.

Most bed-dolls are not found in good condition: Dirty cloth faces, cracking composition finish, soiled clothing or no clothing, and missing parts are normal. If you do buy a "junker," don't pay much. If you can't repair the doll, you don't want it. If you spend a lot of time to rebuild and recostume a doll, it still will never have a high value because it is a restoration. A good rule of thumb is that the total combined price for all the various parts of a doll should never add up to more than the price of a whole doll in average condition.

Pricing Specifics

If you want to have prime examples of the genre, look for Lenci, smokers, painted silk mask-face dolls in elegant or unusual costumes, or more complex bodies with joints. Here is a short list of a very general set of ranges that reflects pricing in the last ten years.

❖ Felt, jointed Lenci, clean with original clothing, no moth holes: $800–$1,500; if exceptional character in fine condition, up to an additional $1,000

❖ Exceptional or unusual piece, such as fully jointed composition smoker in good condition with original clothing: $400–$900, more for mint condition

❖ Cloth (silk or cotton) painted face, in good condition with original clothing: $150–$350; more if unusual or marked

❖ Composition head, arms, legs, in good condition with original clothing: $100–$200; smoker with hole in mouth to hold cigarette, slightly higher (prices for smoker dolls tend to increase as smoking population decreases)

❖ Identifiable type, such as Anita face or Blossom in good condition: $150–$250 and up

❖ Repairs: If you can clean it or patch it without the repair showing, or if you can clean and repair original clothing: $35 (no clothing, dirty, no hair) to $100 (restorable clothing, wig, cleanable body)

This rare and unusual all-original Cubeb smoker could possibly be a prototype. Photo by Pat Brill

Caveat Emptor!

It is often said that the price of an item sold should determine market price. Remember that prices reflect who was there and what they, as individual collectors, wanted to buy. Some days the person who wants a Lenci doll stays home and a person who knows nothing about Lenci dolls has no competition and gets one very much under the going price. The same thing can happen in reverse. Auctions, especially, are a form of gambling. You bet *with your money* that your price will win. The key to winning and being a smart shopper is to stay informed and be knowledgeable. Ask questions and read all the information available. Based on your knowledge, set your own limit and stick to it—even if it means you lose a bid or a purchase opportunity.

For instance, if I see a doll I want—at an auction, a doll show, or on the Internet—I first consider what I know the price range for a good one of that type should be. Then, I consider the item with regard to my collection. I ask myself a series of questions:

❖ Do I need one of those?

❖ How many of those would I want?

❖ Would I be able to sell it the day after for what I paid?

❖ How much work would have to be done to fix it?

❖ How much time do I want to put in and what would its value be after I did the work?

At an auction, I'm especially cautious about bidding on an item. I set my personal limit at what I would pay if I were buying in a shop or show. I have lost a few bids this way—for dolls I really liked—but I didn't lose any money. I put those losses down to learning experiences: I learned that either some people with more money than sense were bidding, or I misjudged the desirability of the item. I can't have them all, but I surely can have fun playing the shopping game.

This Blossom lady is just waiting for a collector to take her home and display her—she's all ready, waiting in her chair. Photo by Pat Brill

Terminology

Terms that Identify Condition or Value

All original (AO):

The doll is in its original costume, has its original wig, and has not been restored or repaired. It might have had a small item replaced, such as a shoelace, button, or hair ribbon, but in most cases it will be as it was sold originally. Condition is usually very good to mint condition. These still command the highest prices even if they are dusty and have melting fabrics.

Marked:

Impressed with a stamp with the manufacturer's name or mark. In some cases, this includes mold or batch numbers. Marks are usually found on the back of the head, shoulders, or center back.

Mint or Mint-in-box (MIB):

A doll that appears just as it came from the factory: unchanged, complete, clean, and crisp; in the original packaging.

Restored or repaired:

The doll has some damage, from missing parts to major deterioration, and there has been some repair work done. This can be a little or a lot, typically repainting or replacing costumes or body parts. A well-done, almost invisible repair or a small first-class restoration does not detract much from price. If the repair shows or if the doll has been dressed with modern fabrics, its value is much lower.

Tagged:

There is a cloth tag sewn into a seam or onto the body of the doll. A hangtag, which is rare, might be attached to the doll's wrist.

Vintage:

The costume fabric and body construction is datable to the original era, even if it was homemade.

Terms that Identify Types

French:

Dolls that are—or dolls that *look* like they are—known to be of French manufacture. In most cases, the term French-type refers to painted silk or cloth faces of exceptionally nice quality, which implies elegant or dainty workmanship and features.

"— Type":

This is simply shorthand for "we don't know for sure it is one." Often, a doll might be called an Anita-type if it resembles the long-faced Anita doll, or it might be referred to as a Blossom-type if it has a more rounded cloth face with fringed eyelashes.

German:

Typically, German dolls are those with flocked pressed paper heads, but the term also often refers to character dolls—clowns, ethnic, or theatrical types. During the 1920s and into the 1930s, German manufacturers were still working with bisque. They also manufactured dolls with bisque heads on pressed-paper or papier-mâché bodies. Bright eyes with nicely painted highlights are a classic characteristic of this type.

TERMS THAT DESCRIBE CONSTRUCTION

Breastplate or shoulder plate:

Usually cast with composition head as one part, the breastplate includes the doll's upper chest and sometimes the breasts.

Bubbles:

These form when the glue holding the cloth-covering on a mask face loosens, and the fabric lifts away.

Button joints or metal joints:

A pair of buttons or metal disks hold two parts of a doll body together, usually the head and/or the limbs. These are fastened by clamping or pinning to the body parts.

Cloth or stuffed cloth:

This describes the material that the doll's body is made of. Usually, this is woven cotton or twill; or sometimes felt.

Composition:

Composition dolls have bodies or body parts made of sawdust, paper maché or bits of cardboard—or all of those—held together with a glue binding. Manufacturers used a number of different mixtures. Doll parts made of composition are hard, painted all over, and very subject to cracking or grazing when exposed to varying temperatures and humidity.

Crazing or grazing:

Light spiderweb cracking that appears when the paint on a composition head lifts away from the molded base and/or the composition shrinks away from the very thick layer of surface paint. Unless stabilized, this is usually followed by major cracking.

Flange head, turn-head, swivel head:

The head is mounted on the breastplate and jointed so that it can turn. This is different from a turned head, which refers to a head sculpted in a fixed, sideways-looking position.

Inset:

Eyes or jeweled embellishments glued into cut-out areas of a head made of composition material.

Mask face, molded face, pressed face or head:

A piece of fabric is glued over a cast, or molded, base form, usually of papier-mâché, but sometimes composition. Earlier mask-face dolls are often very nicely hand-painted, sometimes with oils. Some mask faces had printed face designs.

Melting or shattering:

Damage to aging silk fibers, where the costume fabric appears to be pulling apart or fraying.

Molded-on:

This usually refers to legs where the shoe is sculpted as one with the leg.

Pin joints:

Found on wood and composition doll bodies, a pin joint interlocks like a mortise and tenon and is held in place with a pin.

Rubs:

When the surface of a doll has lost color due to wear, but the surface has not cracked or grazed.

Sleep-eye:

Eyes that have lids and that open and shut.

Stuffing:

The material a cloth body is filled with, usually dark-colored cotton waste, cotton, or occasionally kapok or wool.

Sweetie Pie, a vintage cloth doll, has very special embroidered shoes. Photos by W. Donald Smith

An unusually rare early bed-doll; if you look closely, you will see she has an inset jeweled necklace. Photo by W. Donald Smith

Dolls made between 1920 and 1940

❖ Better painted, more colors, more details
❖ Brush strokes are sharper, eyebrows are thinner
❖ Eyes look to the side in flirty "vamp" looks
❖ Lips are thinner; mouths are cupid's-bow shaped
❖ Bodies have very long, straight cloth limbs
❖ Feet have high-heel shoes that tie at the ankle
❖ Cloth face mask (most were made prior to 1940)
❖ Better grade and finer weave of cloth for face
❖ Homemade-look, roughly applied mask-type cloth face
❖ Inset jewels and glass eyes
❖ Wax, felt, silk, or composition figure
❖ "Art" figures, such as clowns and characters

Rare *Lilli Baitz* wax doll kit with original protective tissue wrapping and sticker. Completed, this doll might have been a telephone cover, an elegant pincushion, or even a lamp base.
Photo by W. Donald Smith

Dolls made between mid-1930s and late 1940s

❖ Faces minimally colored, no eye shadow
❖ Round eyes that look straight ahead
❖ Big "blobby" lips
❖ Composition or plastic limbs on shorter, wider cloth body
❖ Shorter arms and legs
❖ Full, curvy bust, sometimes padded
❖ Black pump-style shoes, molded as one with leg
❖ Cheesecloth faces; poor-quality fabrics and trims
❖ Costumes with full, ruffled skirts; broad-brimmed hats; little or no hair under hat

Until the 1950s, bed-dolls were often sold as heads alone or as kits. An "all-original" bed-doll could very well be made from a purchased mask face, composition head, or a kit; many came with a pattern to use with your own fabrics. Some kits also included costume fabrics and shoes. You could mail order a complete kit for $1.50! In most cases, it's obvious which dolls involved home sewing and assembly, and which were constructed at the factory; if construction and costuming are well done, the homemade doll can be as worthy an example as the manufactured one. By the 1950s, just about any bunch of parts could be assembled and dressed with a long skirt and called a bed-doll.

Fabulous Faces

Without doubt, it's the infinite variety of character expressed in the faces of the bed-dolls that attracts us to them. Cute, funny, vampy, haughty, sly, sad, or just beautiful, the expressions are unique to the style of the era. We just don't see the like in our times. Many of the dolls shown in this gallery are marked and tagged, so study them carefully and use their characteristics as clues when you have a doll you want to identify.

This all-original doll is tagged **"Chas. Bloom"** and dated June 2, 1925. Dolls like this one are known for their very "deco" eyes. Her body is made so that a wind-up music box can be inserted.
Photo by Pat Brill

Here is a pair of all-cloth American beauties. The platinum blonde doll on the left is a tagged Gerling *Hotsy Totsy*. The darker blonde doll on the right is not tagged, but she is believed to be an Etta. At first glance, these two dolls appear to be from the same maker—they both have silk face masks and inset eyelashes. Careful study, however, shows very different body construction and facial molding. Photo by Pat Brill

Not all bed-dolls are vamps. This one looks to be a sweet, likable personality. She is made of suede. Her owner thinks she might be Italian; perhaps because of her hair combs? Photo by Pat Brill

This classic Anita smoker has the ruby-red lips and side-long glance of a true vamp. Her coiled braids and arched eyebrows are typical of this type of doll. Photo by Pat Brill

Another all-original doll, this one tagged *"Gerling."* One of her best features is her carefully painted eyelashes. Her green dress is made from a heavy iridescent silk. Photo by Pat Brill

Here's mystery! This doll's familiar look might lead you to think she is the **Hotsy-Totsy** made by Gerling, but she has a sewn-in tag that says she is an original *Kuddles Toy* by the Jane Gray Company of New York City. Her elegant wine-colored silk dress was painstakingly reconstructed using as much of the original trimming as possible. The gathered skirt was made by running a cord through a sewn casing, a typical method for reducing bulk at the waist. Photo by W. Donald Smith

Poupee Gerb's faces are quite distinct, and extremely lovely. This one's fur hat trim and hair curls at the ears accentuate her delicate features. Photo by Pat Brill

This prim and proper all-cloth doll was made by the American Stuffed Novelty Company. The dolls from this company have a more ladylike appearance than many of their contemporaries.
Photo by Pat Brill

This all-original tagged Etta is wearing very deco lounging pajamas. Ettas were manufactured only from 1927 to 1930. Photo by Pat Brill

Amazing Anita

When the boudoir doll fad hit the United States, The Anita Novelty Company of New York came up with a winning design. Once they saw its popularity, they adapted the doll's basic design into a number of different formats: the economy model of head only; a fold-up body; and dressed as a costume character. When the doll has a large head and an open mouth, it is referred to as an Anita "big-head." The version with a jointed head, referred to by collectors as a "turn-head," was strung with a rubber band held into the chest with a dowel. The more prized common Anitas are the ones with highly colored facial features and "telephone receiver" coiled braids over the ears.

This pristine doll in mint condition is a lovely example of an Anita turn-head. Her underclothes and construction are almost the same as her undressed "sister" on page 53.
Photo by Diane Mardis

A wonderful composition Anita doll head on an original cloth body. The hands are tucked to show the suggestion of a thumb only. Costume is old, but may not be original to the doll. Photo by Maralyn Christoffersen

This Anita turn-head has a lovely face in very good condition. Her bright purple dress belies her innocent look, though—beneath that drab hat, there's a spark of spunkiness!
Photo by Pat Brill

One of the many unusual features of the Anita turn-head is the open mouth with teeth showing. This doll is quite valuable: Notice the clear outline of her nipples, which indicates she came out of a good, clean mold, as did her sister with the garland in her hair on page 52. Even her back is beautiful, and it offers a wonderful view of the construction of her turn-head. This sweetie wears her original bloomers; perhaps she was a lingerie model! Her legs are covered with velveteen or suede fabric. Photos by Maralyn Christoffersen

Rosalinde

Rosalinde, Rosalinde, who is Rosalinde? Each of these dolls has been found with the name Rosalinde written on the foot—either on the side of her little kid shoe, or on a paper label on the shoe. We think they were the work of a smaller group of French artisans. Their 36"-long bodies are made of linen, and they have more anatomical detail than is really necessary for costuming. This is typical of more painstaking artist studio production. The faces are very delicately oil-painted, with enough difference between them all to demonstrate concern for creating individual characters for each type—and perhaps even for each doll. Were they one-of-a-kind? Each one is meticulously fashioned in historical or court costume. It is a fortunate collection, indeed, that can boast of one of these fine examples.

Rosalinde, dressed as Marie Antoinette.
Photo by Diane Mardis

Rosalinde, caught undressed while in the process of being restored. You can clearly see her unique bust construction and her intricate silk floss hairstyle. Photo by Maralyn Christoffersen

Rosalinde, in Spanish Court costume. The stupendous hairstyle shown in detail above is apparently arranged over a wire frame. Her clothes are original, as are her drop jewels. This doll has a paper label on her foot. Photo by Diane Mardis

The Fashionable French Doll

While the Art Deco age was one of short skirts, speedy cars, and bathtub gin, there was still a feeling of nostalgia for the bygone days of romance and elegance. The first bed-dolls to appear on the scene were often costumed in ornate court styles like these. Others were reminiscent of the "cast-of-thousands" historical movie epics and costume musical extravaganzas that were so wildly popular.

A French doll from Belgium according to her tag. And every ruffle and curl all original. Photo by Bonnie Groves

This Marie Antoinette look-alike, is dressed in an elegant silver and lavender gown. Photo by Pat Brill

The Marie Antoinette elegant fashions of the eighteenth century were very popular in 1920s doll circles. The costume of this doll is melting by the moment, so her owner will copy it exactly. Although this particular doll looks very much like the French-made **Les Poupees Gerb's** ladies, a *Lady's Home Journal* article from December 1924 indicates that faces like this one were also made for the home seamstress to complete and costume. Photo by W. Donald Smith

Ooh, la, la—what a costume! Yards of gathered velvet panels are divided by strips of ribbon and lace. This extraordinary confection of a costume is worn by a doll made of wax over composition. Photo by Pat Brill

This poor doll lost her original costume years ago. Her new owner took the time to make an elegant replacement ensemble from yellow moiré taffeta, vintage lace, antique pearls, and handmade silk ribbon roses. The result was worth the effort: This very pretty German-type composition doll now looks like an Italian opera star…and has definitely attracted the attention of a small cloth Italian souvenir doll. Photo by W. Donald Smith

South of the Border

This 32" doll has a felt face, all-felt clothing, and lots of colorful felt detailing—including high-heeled shoes. A well-made piece, she even has wired fingers for posing. She is probably not a Lenci, but she may be from one of the Brazilian makers. Photos by Diane Mardis

This southwestern Spanish couple stand 32" tall. They are made of felt and have a wealth of detail in their costumes. Her blouse is as highly embroidered as his shirt, and his gaucho-style pants have stud decorations all the way down to his boots. Their owner thinks they were made in the late 1920s or early 1930s.

Photos by Diane Mardis

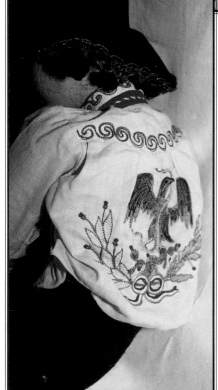

This doll is a Lenci: Her owner found an old company catalog that shows her. She is one of the earlier, more portrait-like characters. Note the wonderful embroidered detail on her shoes. Photos by Diane Mardis

Commédia de l'Arte

Anything representing early theater was fair game for bed-doll theme material. The most frequently found are the *commédia* figures of Pierrot and Pierrette, the boy and girl clowns in black and white; Harlequin, in his diamond-patterned costume; and sometimes Columbine. They are awesomely expressive, but are rarely funny in the humorous sense. Why? Perhaps they reflect a little too much of the sadness underlying crazy modern life. Not surprisingly, because this style of clown suggests playing card designs, we often find that theme as well. Card parties were what kept a lady with spare time occupied during the afternoon. Making bridge tallies and table decorations for her next card party could well have filled her morning.

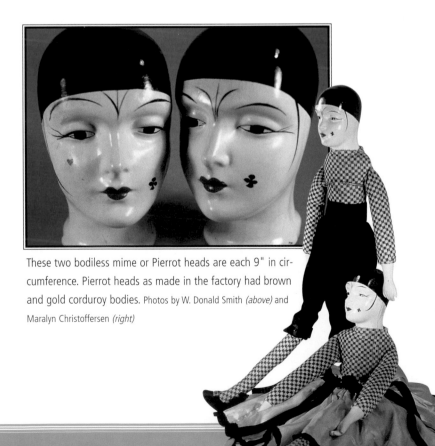

In the Art Deco period, the theatrical characters of the *Commédia de l'Arte* were very popular doll themes. This felt **Pierrot** seems to be Italian, perhaps made by the Alma Company, who manufactured many fine toy dolls during the era. Photo by Pat Brill

These two bodiless mime or Pierrot heads are each 9" in circumference. Pierrot heads as made in the factory had brown and gold corduroy bodies. Photos by W. Donald Smith *(above)* and Maralyn Christoffersen *(right)*

Unfortunately, not all clothing holds up for 80 or 90 years, especially the fragile velvets and silks. These two early Pierrots have had parts of their costumes replaced, but they are still wearing their original caps, shoes, buttons, and lace ruffs. Photo by Diane Mardis

This small (only 17") but thoughtful early French Pierette has a velvet body and velvet painted face. Photo by Pat Brill

Hat stands for the dressing table were made throughout the 1920s. Some even had faces that were better than those of many dolls. This one has a head made of a hard, chalk-like material with a painted face. Photo by Diane Mardis

This all-original Lenci Pierrot is in wonderful condition. He's backstage, waiting to play his mandolin. Photo by Diane Mardis

Not all clowns were Pierrots; this 21" composition and cloth doll looks more like someone dressed in a clownish costume. Dolls with similar features have been found with tags identifying the manufacturer as the German firm of Schelhorn. Photo by W. Donald Smith

Café Society

These smokers are the street-smart tough-guys of doll society.

These street toughs are known around town as the ***"Motley Duo."*** The figure on the left is really *"la Garçonne"*—a lady dressed *à la Bohème* in men's clothing. Street life, even hanging around cafés all day, wasn't always lightness and frills. The bully on the right isn't the type to pass up a fight; check out his black eye as proof positive. Photos by Pat Brill

Catering to the movie mania of the era, many dolls were made to resemble screen stars. This gentleman with oil-painted features does look a bit like a young Bing Crosby. Check him out—he's an all-original cloth bed-doll. His Blossom smoker companion may be a star, too—but which one? Similar types have commanded very high prices. Photo by Pat Brill

Repairing Your Dolls

Art-dolls of the 1920s were made from any one of several materials, including most commonly fabric, wood, and wax. The "true" or "common" bed-doll—the one most likely to be found in dilapidated condition—is usually either cloth or painted composition.

Damage to these bed-dolls dolls is often great, which is why their prices are not really high—or shouldn't be. Cloth dolls suffer from mold; water spotting; rust marks; sun fading; rat, mouse, and moth bites; and sawdust leaks. Composition dolls suffer from grazing, paint chipping, broken or missing parts, dirt, and all the body problems that cloth dolls have. Both types are lucky to have any original hair; if they do, it usually needs to be at least restyled.

You really have to love dolls to take on some of the worst of these basket cases. You also have to realize that, at best, some can be fixed up only to the playable state; they might never become valuable collectibles. Many of the dolls whose photos you see in this book have been cleaned up and restored by their owners. It is amazing how a little bit of your time can give these girls a new look—and they love it.

With any doll restoration, you need to remember that the idea is *restoring,* not *remaking.* An old doll with a new body, a head that has been sanded and repainted, and a brand-new nylon wig is not considered a repaired antique. It now falls into the category of a modern remake. Antique means old. If you take away all the old stuff and replace it, you get new. Like doctors, the

Bubbles (left) is a painted composition doll with an Anita-type face and cloth body. *Costanza (center)* is a mask-face cloth doll, probably made from a purchased kit. *Agnes Ayres (right)* is a painted mask-face doll with a swivel head. All are waiting to be restored; Agnes definitely looks like she expects preferential treatment. Photo by W. Donald Smith

doll restorer should follow the basic rule of "do no harm." However, where a physician makes it better, the doll doctor wants only to stabilize it, as near to original condition as possible. On the other hand, if you're interested in experimenting, go ahead and have your way with your doll. Just don't remake a doll with the idea that it will be worth top dollar when you're done—it never will.

The amount of cleaning you do is a matter of personal choice. Some collectors really love bed-dolls for their tattered, tired look; some

enjoy restoring the old girls to their former glory. I fall in between—it depends on the doll. Sometimes the doll's state requires you do some stabilizing. Sometimes, if you don't spend too much on the doll, it's fun to play around with it to see what happens. I personally don't care for repair jobs that replace old fabrics, trims, and wigs with new synthetic things. To me, this defeats the purpose of enjoying the dolls as historical phenomena.

Here are **Agnes** and **Bubbles,** cleaned, restored, and costumed. What a difference…even Agnes looks a little less touchy. Photo by W. Donald Smith

SIMPLE REPAIRS

Always begin any repair job with the least intrusive treatment. As you see progress, you can use more and more aggressive methods—but remember less is more in this case.

Vacuum:
Often a doll comes to you in pretty good shape, but it looks a little dull. This is often just plain dirt and dust. Start with a simple vacuum treatment. Use a rubber band to secure a piece of nylon stocking over the end of your vacuum cleaner hose. Vacuum the doll from head to toe, including the hair and

inside all the folds of the clothes. Do not use the brush—that only pushes the dirt further into the fabric. If this seems to do the trick, press her clothes and put her on display.

Erase:
If the doll is still soiled after vacuuming, the next step is the eraser. Not just any old eraser—an art gum eraser. Your best bet is to visit an art and drafting supply store, where you can buy bagged art gum eraser material, often called a "scummy bag." Architects and draftsmen like this because it is easy to hold and can work a larger surface. Go over the surface of a dusty or dirty cloth, felt, or

composition doll with the art gum eraser for amazing results. Be careful to rub softly so you remove only the dirt.

Launder:
If the clothing is still soiled, you'll need to remove it from the doll. Keep a pair of pliers handy to pull out any staples or pins. The rule of thumb here is to go cautiously and carefully. Most cleaning products will tell you to check fabrics for colorfastness before using, and you absolutely must do this. Use a corner of the fabric that is not likely to show. Wet the fabric, and press it between two white paper towels. If any color comes off on the paper towels, proceed with extreme caution. These colors may come clean, but expect them to fade: orange to apricot, turquoise to pale blue, and rose to pink. Colored trim on the clothing can also run; you'll want to remove any lace or other trims before laundering. If you suspect cotton might shrink, use lukewarm water, and stretch the fabric out flat on a towel to dry. Press and reshape the garments before the fabric is completely dry.

Remove stains:
Stubborn stains, such as food or crayon, can often be removed with Perk!, a product formulated for cleaning doll clothes and parts. Follow the manufacturer's instructions for stain removal. Another typical fabric damage comes from rust stains—not the metal rust we usually think of, but the result of condensation where pollutants on the fabric combine with moisture. This is often sap from wooden boxes or furniture. Treat these rust stains with a paste made of equal parts salt, water, and cream of tartar. Work the paste into the stain, let it dry, and brush it off. Repeat as necessary.

Whiten:
Bleach is bad news! Never use chlorine bleach—or a product containing it—on dolls or doll clothes. If you need to lighten, use a non-chlorine whitening agent. Doll repair people use Oxyclean, Biz, and even Efferdent. Always test for colorfastness in a hidden spot before trying any product on a whole garment.

Treat specialty fabrics specially:
With many delicate fabrics, you need to use techniques that insure you don't ruin the texture, color, or look.

❖ Clean satin and taffeta with mild detergent

❖ Treat felt, which usually has a high wool content, as you would a sweater: Use cool water and lay flat to dry

❖ To recondition velvet, vacuum, steam, and then brush

❖ Shampoo wigs or wig materials just as you would your own hair, but use lukewarm water, especially if the material is synthetic

❖ Use Oxyclean or detergent to wash colorfast yarn wigs

❖ Clean silk faces with a fresh eraser and work very, very gently—never wash them

Clean the body:
Most cloth dolls and all costumes are made of sized, never-washed fabrics. While some experts say that a cloth or felt doll can be washed, others would never try it. When washed, many fabrics become very soft. Once water is in the fabric, it can cause water spots—usually little wave patterns—if it is not thoroughly worked through all parts, rinsed out well and dried carefully. Most cloth stuffed dolls of the era were packed with gray

waste cotton, so they look frightful when wet. If you decide to wash your doll, there are a number of upholstery cleaners, dog shampoos, and other chemical cleaners that would probably work. All of these contain chemicals, which impregnate the fabric and in the long run, cause deterioration. If you must wash, dilute any detergent with water, and use a piece of sheeting or muslin to gently wipe the surface. Remove all moisture by sponging—never rub!—the surface with a clean cloth.

If I can't get a doll thoroughly clean using the simple processes above, I usually let her be who she is and make up a story to explain it, rather than keep trying and potentially cause even more damage. For instance, the ink stain on Costanza's face (see page 28) is explained away by her job as a secretary; Maria Espidrilla (see page 27) has a darkened face and wears a veil because she was once in a terrible fire. Fortunately, she escaped with her life!

Repair cracks: Cracks in painted
composition dolls often are quite prominent because they have collected dirt, and the result is a dark line or a jigsaw puzzle-looking face or body. I have had good luck by simply wiping the face with a soft cloth just barely dampened with warm water and dish soap. The key word is *wipe:* Do not soak or scrub vigorously. If water gets into the cracks it will lift the paint. Lifting the surface layer of grime will brighten up your doll considerably, but it leaves behind the worst of the dark cracks. I have used a couple of techniques on these:

❖ Flesh-colored acrylic paint: Put a drop or two on your fingertip and work it into the crack lines; wipe off any paint that gets onto surrounding areas—you want paint only in the crack itself; if the crack is through eye or cheek color, use matching paint

❖ Wright's silver polish: On composition faces, remove grime and fill in cracks by applying the polish sparingly; do not rub

❖ Clear wax polishes: Restore the original shine with a light application—this very, very simple method can be just the quick fix-up your gal needs

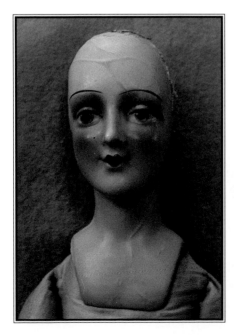

Many dolls are found in the same condition as poor **Bubbles,** shown here *(left)* after her hair was removed. They are impossible to repair without totally repainting and replacing the hair and costume, which many collectors might consider not worth the effort. Bubbles cleaned up nicely, though—you could say she's a whole new woman *(right).* She's changed her ways, too. Although you can still see the surgical repair to her forehead, she has sworn off knife fights entirely. Photos by W. Donald Smith

Rebuilding Parts

Broken fingers or missing limbs can easily be rebuilt with a little patience. Creative Paperclay is a very good product to use. For small parts, model the missing area onto the doll, making a smooth transition at the break. Let the part dry thoroughly, lift it off the doll, spread glue on the areas to be joined, and replace the part. Sand the area lightly if necessary, and paint with flesh-colored paint. Use a light wax to restore the shine. Bed-doll arms and legs are not complex sculptures. If you have one to copy, model a replacement from the air-drying clay, let it dry thoroughly, sand it, and paint as above.

Where large areas of paint over composition have cracked, raised, or peeled, you can cut, carve, or sand the damaged areas until you have a flat surface. Then, rebuild the surface with white Creative Paperclay or Celluclay II, smooth the wet surface with water, and let it dry completely. Sand the surface smooth and even. Paint with matching flesh-tone paints, applying thin coats, and sand between each coat for a brush-stroke-free surface.

𝒩ote: It is interesting that the typical Caucasian flesh-tone paint used for composition doll parts seems to have stayed the same for nearly a century. Lacquer-based doll repair paints available from suppliers almost always match these older gals extremely well. Acrylic craft paints—particularly Delta Ceramcoat Fleshtone—also make a very good match with older painted surfaces.

Rebuilding Cloth Bodies

There are three main situations where you will find yourself restoring or replacing a cloth body:

❖ If your doll has a damaged cloth body with a sewn-on mask face, detach the mask face, if you can do so without causing it to lose its shape. Use the old body as a pattern, and make a whole new body. If the face cannot easily be detached and the body has holes or otherwise needs to be replaced, make a "slipcover" for the old body, and cover over the existing fabric with new.

❖ If you have a mask face without a body, make a body pattern. See the Project section, page 108, for a sample pattern. Design and sew a head back to fit your mask. Sew and assemble the body. Sew the mask face on over the stuffed head. Make sure when you add hair or another head covering that you cover the seam where the mask is attached to the head back.

❖ If you need a partial cloth body to finish off where composition parts end, draw a body pattern, or modify the one from the Project section, page 116. Lay the composition parts on top of the drawn pattern, and make any adjustments needed for size and scale, length of limbs, neck opening, etc. Measure the composition limbs to make sure the sewn fabric pattern pieces will have openings large enough for the limb ends to fit inside. Since composition parts vary in length, you will have to decide how long the fabric arm and leg portions should be.

Replacing Wigs

Most bed-dolls had simple mohair hairstyles, glued directly to the doll's head. If new hair is needed, use mohair curls or lengths of mohair roving—a twisted roll of mohair, available from doll suppliers. Mohair from a goat—via the doll supplier—is even better. See page 127 for sources of these materials.

To begin, cover the head with plastic wrap. Cut a length of cotton buckram and wrap it around the head so that the edge is above the forehead and runs along the hairline. Pin the buckram in place, dampen it slightly, and make small folded pleats around the head to fit the buckram to the head shape. When it is dry, you will have a stiff fabric wig base. Leave the buckram on the head and handstitch the mohair curls to it, forming the hairstyle. When you're finished, gently lift off the wig, remove the plastic from the head, and glue the wig to the head.

The most desirable bed-dolls have elaborate hairstyles made with silk floss. If your doll's hair is still present, restore the original style by carefully relaying each strand. In very sad cases, this might mean taking the whole hairstyle apart and remaking it. If you think you might not remember how it went, take a photograph or draw the hairstyle first. If only a portion of the original silk floss hair is present, you might want to consider restoring that part as best you can and creating an interesting hat, turban, or headband for the doll. Note that your bed-dolls may have been specifically made to wear a hat or head decoration; often these dolls were never fully wigged even when new. What looks like a bald spot might actually be an area that never had hair because originally it was under a hat.

STORING YOUR "NEW" DOLL

When you have finished restoring and repairing your dolls, never store them in plastic. Plastic wrappings retain moisture from the air, give off gases, and can cause chemical changes in materials stored in close proximity. Trapped moisture causes watermarks and rust stains on cloth, and causes composition to swell and crack. If your dolls must be stored, wrap them in old sheets or buffered archival paper. My

1929 Lenci was stored for sixty years wrapped in tissue paper, and it survived—in mint condition. Modern gift tissues are not safe either: They may contain acids and dyes that can transfer onto your doll. Use only specially made pH-balanced archival tissue papers. For a penny a sheet, it is well worth the price. Look for archival papers at your photo supply or picture framing shop, or scrapbook/craft stores.

REPAIR CASE STUDIES
Case 1: "Agnes Ayres"

Agnes was, indeed, the first of the trio on page 64 to be repaired. Here she is "after." Photo by W. Donald Smith

I spotted Agnes at a doll show, hanging from the end of a display by her few remaining strands of silk-floss hair. She wore a pink cotton "teddy" chemise and a very sad petticoat of grayed lavender netting. Her cloth body was cheap, chintzy fabric stuffed with old gray cotton. Her head, made of cotton stretched over a mask of pressed cardboard, was attached to the body with a button joint. Her face, while fairly clean and unmarked, had a "bashed" nose that was askew—almost as if a boyfriend had beaten her up. Gambling on the chance that I could open up her head and work the nose back into its original shape, I purchased her at a substantial "negotiated discount" from the dealer.

About two minutes after getting home, I clipped off Agnes's lavender wig and snipped open the stitches of the head's back seam. Working my way through the cotton head stuffing with the eraser end of a pencil, I was able to push the nose back into its original shape. With the pencil pressed as tightly as possible into the nose depression, I held her face over a steaming teakettle, just a few seconds at a time, just enough to dampen the nose area. (Too much moisture or steam causes water spots on fabric.) With the pencil holding the shape, I let the nose area dry, then added quite a bit more stuffing and stitched the seam closed.

Although Agnes didn't appear too dirty, I knew from experience she would look better with just a little attention. I used a "scummy bag" on her face, and she cleaned up quite nicely. Next, I took off her clothing. A good soaking cleaned up the cotton chemise with no problem. The dilapidated net skirting was risky, but it, too, washed well. As is often the case, the body was soiled along the wrinkle lines. It also smelled of mildew. After some consideration, I decided to take the old gray cotton stuffing out, wash the body fabric, and restuff it.

Essentially, I very nearly rebuilt the whole doll. I could have just made a new body, but Agnes's original body had stitched fingers and the tattered remains of lace and rosette-trimmed shoes that I wanted to preserve. I made her a new costume to go on over her teddy, and I incorporated the lace and rosettes (from her original shoes) into the bottom of her pajama costume. I remade the old lavender netting into a turban.

In all, I spent only an evening restoring Agnes—without losing any more of her originality than necessary.

Case 2: "Nina"

Despite the look on her face, **Nina** is pleased to have a nose repair that's not at all noticeable. Photo by W. Donald Smith

This doll came in a bargain "parts" bag. Her head was just barely hanging onto a pink fabric body that was extremely stinky and mildewed. Phew! Her composition legs had been pulled out of the upper fabric legs, and the stuffing was bursting out. The arms were still attached to the body and needed only a little cleaning up. Nina's real problem was her nose. The paint, along with a little of the underlying composition, was chipped and worn away quite considerably; definitely a candidate for plastic surgery.

To rebuild Nina's nose, I worked very wet Creative Paperclay into the missing area, smoothing and filling in the original shape. Once it was dry, I sanded it lightly to blend the new nose tip into the old painted composition surface. To match the paint, I used small dots of three different flesh-tone acrylics and blended the color into the new nose with my fingertip. If you looked closely, you could see that a repair had been made, so I used a trick to disguise the tiny remaining surface irregularity: lighting. I covered the face with a piece of paper, leaving just the end of the nose sticking out, then I sprayed the nose lightly with a matte sealer. The sealer has just enough gloss to reflect light off the face, making the surface look consistently smooth and even. A pro could probably get a smoother application right away with an airbrush.

In Nina's case, the body was nothing rare and extraordinary to be saved, so I tossed it out and reassembled her on a new body. It was definitely easier to do…and a lot easier on the noses of those who might get close to her!

Case 3: "Paulette"

Paulette's new costume is made with vintage fabrics and trims. Her new makeup closely resembles her original appearance. Photos by W. Donald Smith

Paulette was at an antique show, and she appeared to be suffering from a bad case of scarring, which did nothing for her very flirty expression. Little holes all over her face made her look as if she had survived a bad case of chicken pox. She came with an original wig that appeared to be gray human hair, and her original ribbon flower hair ornament was intact. For ten dollars, I thought I could afford to play.

I removed Paulette's wig, wiped her face, and began to dab flesh-colored paint into the pockmarks on her face. Her original cheek color had been airbrushed, which can make it very difficult to blend repair paint at the edges. However, I managed to match the color and blotted it on. I used a fine-tip paintbrush to fill in the missing portions of her eyebrows, eyeliner, and lip color.

Because so much of her face was repainted, I resorted to a little trickery to pull off a well-blended look: I gave Paulette two beauty spots to distract the eye from the irregularities. When the face was done, I sprayed the whole head with a gloss spray finish to make the surface appear blended. The result is a head that has essentially been redone but retains the flavor of the era with nearly seventy percent of the original face color.

I do stress that this is something I did only because I considered this to be a doll with "throw-away" parts. I would never try this on an otherwise reasonable doll, nor would I ever attempt to pass off such a repair/remake as an original.

Case 4: "Rinalda"

Rinalda—restored. Her face seems to be flocked felt and her hair is silk floss. She has a wonderfully well-preserved, Lenci-like, jointed felt body with separate fingers. A little tiny sticker on her leg says simply, "Brazil." Photo by W. Donald Smith

I had just promised myself, "No more big dolls," then Rinalda arrived in the form of a photo and a phone call from a friend who wanted to sell her. A check in the mail later and she was in my workshop, in need of major help. Although she had all her original clothing and trimmings, everything, with the exception of her body and her blue organdy undies, was in a rather poor state.

To fix her up and still preserve all the original elements required almost remaking her costume. I removed, washed, pressed, refolded, and reattached her headdress of shattered silk. A few additional painted wooden fruits (as well as the little banana man) helped fill out her head basket. I added a dab of paint as a quick fix for her eye, and I carefully redid her hair to hide a large piece of missing face covering. I laundered and pressed her blouse and scarf right away. But it took almost a year to match the green taffeta so I could make her a new skirt, which incorporates the original lace inserts and their felt zigzag trim, as well as the large felt flowers. It was a simple matter to rejuvenate the old, faded flowers: I took each flower apart carefully, then reassembled each one with the brighter side of the felt facing up. I did have to replace the zigzag felt trim around her skirt, and one heel of her carved wooden shoes. All back together, she is as good as new…almost.

Repair Stories

Here's a challenge—or an opportunity. This head is cracked, mildewed, and chipped …but can you imagine all her possibilities? After all she's been through, this doll still smiles serenely, as if she trusts you implicitly to transform her into just the right person. A little careful cleaning, a dab of paint here and there, and the endless costume possibilities will make your head swim. Photo by author

Sally Ann's face has been partially cleaned using an art gum eraser. Her dirty composition face is coming remarkably clean with this gentle treatment—you can see the clean streaks on her right cheek. Photo by W. Donald Smith

Half-dolls were—and still are—very popular collector's items. These two painted plaster ladies *(left)* display typical poses. They were originally dressed in green oilcloth and attached to large plaster baskets, probably for use as table decorations. Removed, cleaned up, dressed, wigged, and hatted, they're displayed beautifully on these brass candlesticks *(right)*.
Photo by W. Donald Smith

Arlette the Coquette is contemplating fabrics for a new costume that will match her eyes. Her head was most likely a purchased part; as you can see, someone tried hard to make a body with a ladylike figure—most likely not for this head. This "marriage" of mismatched, in shape and scale, body and head is fairly typical of many dolls you'll find. What to do? It's the owner's choice—you can make a more "correct,"—but not original—body, or work with what is there. What I like about Arlette is that she tells us that not all our grandmothers were wonderful seamstresses. Photo by W. Donald Smith

Collectors of bed-dolls often take liberties with costumes. This doll seems to be a Gerling, but the costume may have originally belonged to another doll. Although it fits nearly perfectly, it has an added pink organdy neck insert that someone used to cover the cloth torso where it peeked through above the neckline.(See page 62 for a more detailed photo of her small companion.) Photo by W. Donald Smith

This rare doll has both glass eyes and human hair. As it became more labor intensive and costly during the 1920s to include these features, fewer and fewer were made. Today, finding one is a rare treat. The owner of this gal used her sewing machine's ruffling attachment to create an authentic-looking costume. Photo by W. Donald Smith

The Zaga of Zona

No bed-doll book I could write would be complete without the Zaga of Zona…or at least some of it.

When a few of us began to collect, make, and tell stories about bed-dolls, our friend Delores didn't have one. She got in the game anyway by making up the story of Zona, The Prodigal Girl, creating her personality through postcards and letters (and police reports) that showed up in Delores's mailbox. As time went on, Delores "discovered" that Zona had two sisters, but none of them ever came home. Zona had grown away from her family.

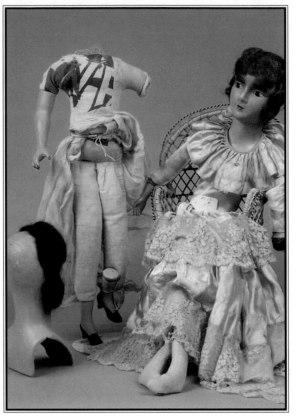

We were all going to a doll conference when one of us found a really cheap, extremely dilapidated bed-doll in a thrift shop. She bought it for Delores and we began to make plans for a grand presentation. At the conference, I had a seminar to do for the whole group—about 500 collectors. At the end of my talk, I was handed an envelope by one of my co-conspirators. From the podium I read the message to Delores. It said, "I am really, really sorry and want to come home. Please meet me in the hotel lobby florist shop. Signed, Your loving Zona."

Delores, followed by at least a hundred curious conventioneers, hotfooted it to the shop. There on a shelf was the most tatty, hairless, disreputable looking, one-armed bed-doll you ever did see. She was sitting on the shelf with a note pinned to her that explained her condition— "due to riotous living and a poor choice of boyfriends." She begged to be forgiven. Delores was delighted and the game began in earnest.

Just before dinner on Friday night, a hotel clerk paged Delores. (Bed-dolls do make things happen in your life.) Apparently Zona had asked the clerk to leave a note for Delores. The note told Delores that Zona, bored with sitting around in the hotel room, had gone off with the bartender from the hotel lounge. Delores thought this was another gag note, but I said, "No, this means Zona is gone. She won't be in the room when we get there." Sure enough, she

Here is **Zona's** original body and head *(left)* alongside her more attractive (and intact) sister. No wonder she hates her sister!
Photo by W. Donald Smith

wasn't. Delores had a real look of consternation; it is not at all funny when someone takes away your doll! Delores played along, but anxiously wondered what would happen next.

The next day another note, this time from Zona herself, was delivered to Delores. Zona was leaving a trail of disaster. The bartender had abandoned her! Zona told Delores to meet her in the bar at 11:00 p.m.

That night, Delores and about twenty curious friends went to the hotel bar. There was Zona, draped over the bar in even more disarray than usual, with empty glasses, spilled drinks, and filled ashtrays around her. Zona had plainly had it. We were going to let her sleep it off, but next thing we knew she was up and dancing with the fellows, flirting with the band players, and table-hopping. Obviously Zona was on the prowl again. Delores decided that enough was enough. She said goodnight and turned to collect Zona from her barstool. But Zona was gone again!

Sunday morning we went to brunch and prepared for the long drive home. Delores was sure that Zona would show up before we left, but no Zona—not even a note this time. As we left, Delores warned, "If anyone sees that little no-good on the road, don't pick her up. She is disowned!" We passed a military convoy going

by Yakima, so it was not surprising when, the next evening at a doll club meeting, Delores answered the doorbell to find Zona on the porch, escorted by two teddy bears in full uniform. Zona had been picked up in the Yakima military reserve, but was being returned because not even a regiment of Green *Bear*ets could handle her.

Zona is now "resting at home." She has been reunited with her sisters Zenith and Zelda (whom she hates because they are in much better physical shape). Even so, letters from old pal collectors and an attorney followed Zona right to Delores. Delores got a pretty terse letter and a very big bill from a hotel in Cincinnati where Zona was supposedly partying. (It happened there had been a regional doll conference at that hotel the week before the letter arrived . . . the game had moved across country.) I gave Zona a Bible to read, and we're hoping for a conversion to a more restrained lifestyle, but don't count on it. Someone named Otto has been sending her postcards from around the world.

Once she settled in at home, *Zona* became a little more respectable. Here, she's playing the lady *(above)*, and dreaming of future travels to the Orient *(below)*. Photos by W. Donald Smith

The Smoking Gallery

Smoking was a fact, a fad, and a definite 1920s phenomenon. Tobacco use was not a new thing. Along with rum, it was the major profitable and exportable crop in America from 1610 on through the American Revolution and beyond. Men had smoked in public for centuries. Women had smoked, too, but in Queen Victoria's buttoned-up society, women confined it to their bedrooms. In the post-World War I era, smoking in public represented modernity and liberation. It went right along with the radical changes in fashions and hairstyles. Ashtrays abounded, and a good hostess would offer cigarettes to visitors. No one minded and everyone did it.

While some of these dolls aren't the classic "smoker" doll , they represent the smoking fad, and many were made with a mouth that could hold a cigarette. Smokers or smoker "wannabes," they're still all delightful.

If any one doll represents the American Art Deco scene, it is the smoker. These were the girls that had "it" all. The smoker, public and in-your-face, was a symbol of the new post-War society. Not only did their ankles show, but also they wore trousers: thoroughly scandalous (and great fun). How times and social views change! Every collector had to have one, and most still feel a collection is not complete without one or two examples of smokers. Lenci, Cubeb, and Anita were, and still are the most popular.

The classic flapper smoker is the Fadette, with a molded felt face and body, made by Lenci. Photo by Pat Brill

This cigarette girl was made by the European Novelty Company. These dolls are known as Cubebs (for the type cigarette they advertised). Although you can see how the Lenci design influenced the shape of her head and costume design, this cigarette girl is composition. Photos by Pat Brill

A full-face view of a Cubeb dressed in a crepe satin suit with marabou trim. Photo by Pat Brill

Undressed, this Cubeb reveals her pin joints. Photo by Pat Brill

This jointed felt smoker is thought to be a Lenci. Photo by Estelle Johnston

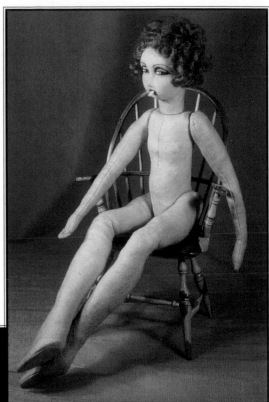

Oh so decadent, this pristine reclining smoker was obtained in her original box from the original owner's grandchild; she had been hidden away in a cedar chest in the cellar. She represents the essential form of the era. Photo by Diane Mardis

Here's the racy jazz-age flapper. Quite the sophisticate, this Lenci Fadette was made in about 1922. She is 26" long, and has a felt mask face and muslin parts. All her joints swivel, and she appears to be stuffed with straw. This doll wears trousers—and probably drives a sporty little roadster, too. Except for her headband, she is all original, and a particularly nice example of her type in mint condition.
Photo by Maralyn Christoffersen

A 32" smoker, this gal is probably an unmarked Lenci, made to represent the famous fashion designer Coco Chanel. She wears her original pink felt clothing, complete with silk stockings, gold cloth purse, and rolled cigarette. Photo by Maralyn Christoffersen

A cloth mask, so-called "silk face" smoker head. The fabric is really more like twill-weave cotton. Notice that the eyes have been glazed to reflect light and to add to her personality. Photo by Maralyn Christoffersen

This 5" composition smoker head has a semi-open mouth that shows a row of teeth. When not having her picture taken, she wears a blonde bobbed wig. This would be a great find for a collector who likes to create characters and costumes. Photo by Estelle Johnston

This composition smoker doll was manufactured to advertise Cubeb-type cigarettes. Her body has been fully restored with original hardware, and her face, head, and wig are original. The Cubeb dolls are thought to have been fashioned after the Lenci Fadette design.

Photo by Estelle Johnston

A German composition smoker head with applied flocking on a velvet body. Photo by Maralyn Christoffersen

This very famous smoker doll wearing a gypsy costume was made by the Blossom Company. Her hair is painted—but only the part that shows. Photos by Maralyn Christoffersen

The Boarders

Madge and her friend Vernonia left teacher's college to go make their fortunes in Hollywood. Little Vernonia became a pretty-face ingénue—giving the famous Mary Pickford a run for her money. Madge looked at things with a more practical viewpoint. She opened a boarding house for ladies in the film industry, and used its profits to invest in orange groves around Los Angeles. You should know that Madge might be trying to quit smoking. I can't tell you how many times she has swallowed her cigarette—so many, anyway, that her head rattles.

Madge Smith, Coed is a smoker who was originally only a head with a raffia collar. She was probably meant to be what was called a cheer stick or mascot, a head or small figure attached to a decorated stick or made to hang from the rear view mirror of a car. When I got her, I made her a body of vintage velveteen and dressed her in the remains of an old ruffled taffeta bedspread. You can see how the addition of the bridge tally, an elaborate oriental knotted tassel, and a mandolin reflect the motifs of the era and add to the collegiate party-girl effect. Purists might argue that I should have kept this head as it was. In this case, I was careful to preserve all the original parts and to use vintage fabrics and embellishments. No matter what, it is still a makeover. The monetary value is only in the original head and the vintage accessories; the rest of the value is in the pleasure she gives me and others who smile at her story.
Photo by W. Donald Smith

Vernonia wasn't the only boarder at Madge's boarding house, which was actually a group of bungalow apartments built around a courtyard. It attracted several ladies from the Hollywood scene.
Photo by W. Donald Smith

Mysterious *Maria Esperanza Espadrilla* is a cloth mask-face doll. We think she wears a veil because she has suffered some smoke damage that darkened her complexion; when meeting new people, she often draws it up over her face. Both Nina and Maria wear clothes made from a shattered vintage 1920s dress. Photo by W. Donald Smith

This is *Nina, the Nose*. Her friends called her that—but not in front of her face—because she works as a cashier in a studio cafeteria, where she collects the local gossip. One day, she stuck her nose so far into a conversation that it got bitten! Nina is an Anita-face doll whose unfortunate nose had to be repaired. Photo by W. Donald Smith

Ivy Fern Greenleaf, the Acrobatic Dancer, was created from a purchased mask face and vintage fabrics. As you might imagine, she is quite the life of the party at the boarding house. Photo by W. Donald Smith

The **Countess Nazimova**, dressed in the remains of a court dress that survived her flight from the ravages of the Russian Revolution to her life in Hollywood, often visits with **Sergei, the Cossack Prince,** to relive old memories. Sergei is a bisque-headed doll on a very-poorly-made composition body. Although he carries severe head wounds (cracks) he has found a new lease on life with the bed-doll ladies. Photo by W. Donald Smith

This is *Lulu, Countess Bomblitzkaya.* She was born Louise Kravitz in Dubuque, Iowa. When she danced as a Ziegfield chorus girl, she changed her name to Lulu Lamont. Later, she eloped with a local famous stagedoor Johnny, the dripping-rich Count Bomblitzkof. The Count, long since gone to his reward, left Lulu rich enough, but she still likes to indulge in writing squibs for the Hollywood gossip columnists. Photo by W. Donald Smith

Making Your Own Dolls

A smashing Blossom smoker relaxes with vintage needlework pillows. Photo by Pat Brill

Getting Started

If you can use a sewing machine and/or do basic hand sewing, you can make an Art Deco doll from cloth following a simple pattern. To insure successful sewing, always read all the information on every pattern before going to work. Be sure to transfer all markings and study the construction details before beginning, and read all the information printed on the pieces themselves.

If you want to make a really authentic-looking doll, study the photos in this book and the illustrations and information in this section to become familiar with Art Deco-style facial features, materials, colors, hairstyles, and so on. Other good resources include fashion and costume books, or magazines from the Art Deco era.

SELECTING BODY FABRIC

Cloth dolls of the Art Deco era were made of plain-woven cotton goods, and sometimes, polished cotton or chintz. It might be difficult to find polished cotton or chintz in a flesh color these days, but keep in mind that some bodies were made in other colors. If you want that shiny look but can't find the color you want, consider painting and glazing the whole body.

The other most commonly-used fabric is felt, an excellent doll-making material. Fabric and craft stores carry several colors that are usable for flesh; you'll find bolts, 1-yard packages, and craft squares. Felt stuffs very smoothly, but a well-stuffed felt piece will be slightly larger than the same piece made in woven goods— important to remember if you're making costumes for the doll.

SELECTING COSTUME FABRIC

Underwear (if they wore any) was either rayon jersey or fine cotton stockinet knit; today's contemporary underwear fabrics are quite similar. Petticoats or underskirts were made of cheesecloth (you can use gauze) or very low-quality muslin.

Dresses were made of silky rayon, taffeta, or satin fabrics; these are similar to contemporary lining fabrics. Fancier costumes used silk or *panné* (velvet), chiffon, or polished cotton, all of which are readily available today. Trims were commonly inexpensive cotton lace, gold lace, or braid—you'll find plenty of these in the trims section of your local fabric or craft store.

Shoes were made of oilcloth, silk, or leather. Look for vinyl tablecloth yardage or painted fabric for your doll. Hats were mostly wide-brimmed, made of dress fabric stiffened with an inner lining of buckram. (Lenci dolls, always the exception, were made of felt and costumed with organdy and felt decorations.)

Important!

Always check your garment pattern pieces against your finished doll body before cutting and sewing. Depending on your individual method of sewing, type of stuffing, and fabric used, there are often variations in doll body size. Cut the pattern pieces from paper towels or napkins, and lay them against the body to make sure they will fit when they are sewn together with the ¼" seam allowance. Paper towels are also a great way to design and test clothing patterns of your own!

Costuming Your Dolls

Many dolls in the 1920s had costumes made from purchased kits like this one. Everything was included—even the shoes and hair. At right is the kit dress as it was made up by the contemporary owner. Photos by W. Donald Smith

This pristine silk-face doll is very typical of bed-doll construction. She has composition limbs and a body of coarse cotton stuffed with cotton waste. As the doll shows no sign of ever having been dressed, it is possible it was purchased ready-made to be dressed by the owner. Photo by W. Donald Smith

Bed-dolls often were purchased undressed. *Goldie* is one of those—a girl just waiting for a new wardrobe.
Photo by W. Donald Smith

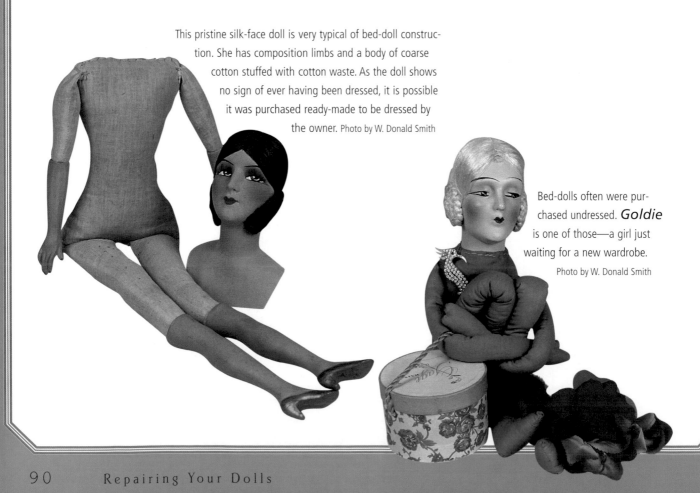

A Few Rules

When creating costumes, I follow a few simple rules that help me find the right fabrics, colors, and accessories—and put them together well—without stifling my own creativity.

1. Dress the doll in something that resembles 1920s bed-doll costuming. There are lots of themes to choose from. Look through this book for ideas, or check out Stephanie Farrago's wonderful book, *The Magic and Romance of Art Dolls.* We tend to think of the bed-doll as a lady in a long, lovely dress, but there were also clowns, Orientals, Blacks, theatrical characters, Spanish dancers, and fantasy, novelty floral, and flapper-vamp types.

2. If you can, use old fabrics. Do not—repeat, *do not*—cut up a good vintage piece to make a costume. When I set about costuming the doll that eventually became Little Vernonia (see page 85), I prematurely decided an old dress, made with alternating bands of beige lace and lavender silk ribbon, was beyond restoring. As soon as I cut into it, I found waist hoop panniers—and I realized much too late I had just destroyed a piece of museum-quality vintage clothing. Had I taken the time to investigate carefully first, I would have taken the time to re-line, restore, and preserve the whole dress as a historical artifact. So, be careful what you cut into. Instead, keep on the lookout for odd pieces of 1920s clothing—such as panels or trim bands from beaded dresses that are already cut—that just beg to be used in a doll's costume. Also, feel free to use any handwork techniques—such as embroidery, silk ribbon work, crochet, and tatting—to enhance your costumes. These are the things that will make your doll look and feel like the old ones.

3. Reconstruct your dolls so they look old. That is, don't make it look like a newly dressed, freshly made piece. I like the idea of faded beauty, and that is what I like to see in my bed-doll crew. I want them to re-create the atmosphere, ambience, and flavor of what it must have been like in the era. Others feel differently; it's a matter of personal taste.

COSTUMING YOUR DOLLS

Before you decide on a costume for any doll—one you buy and restore, or one you make—you should understand the attitudes of the Art Deco era. There were two views of women in the 1920s.

❖ The smart, sophisticated, ultra-modern fashion lady was seen in the costume pages of every ladies' magazine of the era—she stood quite straight—you could almost feel the starch in her backbone and see her swagger

❖ The languid, loose, soft, romantic lady had a droopy head; fluttery, downcast eyes; clasped hands; and legs posed in ballet-like positions

When you re-create your bed-doll, pick a pose that you will carry through the head and body construction and costuming. That way, you will have a doll with a real personality and perhaps be able to tell good story about her.

Choosing Colors

Every era is identified with a certain set of colors. If you want to make your bed-dolls reflect the flapper era use one major color and one or two accent colors. Here are some typical 1920s color combinations:

❖ Red with white and black

❖ Orange with tan, kelly green, or dusty green

❖ Gold with magenta or orange

❖ Lavender with pink, pale green, gold, or black

❖ Turquoise or robin's-egg blue with black or gold

❖ Teal with gray

❖ Magenta with gold or rose

❖ Brown with orange or neutrals

❖ Gray with coral

❖ Silver with gray and taupe

❖ All pastels

Very few dolls wore blue, yellow, or purple. Some dolls wore dusty or mossy greens, but not true green.

CHOOSING A FACE DESIGN

What really makes an Art Deco doll—especially the flapper-vamp bed-doll—is her particular flirty-eyed look. Some of these girls are very wide-eyed, and some wear pretend-sexy side glances. Their eyebrows are nicely arched curves or almost straight lines, and they wear their eyelashes long. Mouths on dolls of the 1920s are little cupid's bows, but dolls from the 1930s have a slightly larger lip line. Use the examples below to experiment with mixing and matching features to create your own dolls.

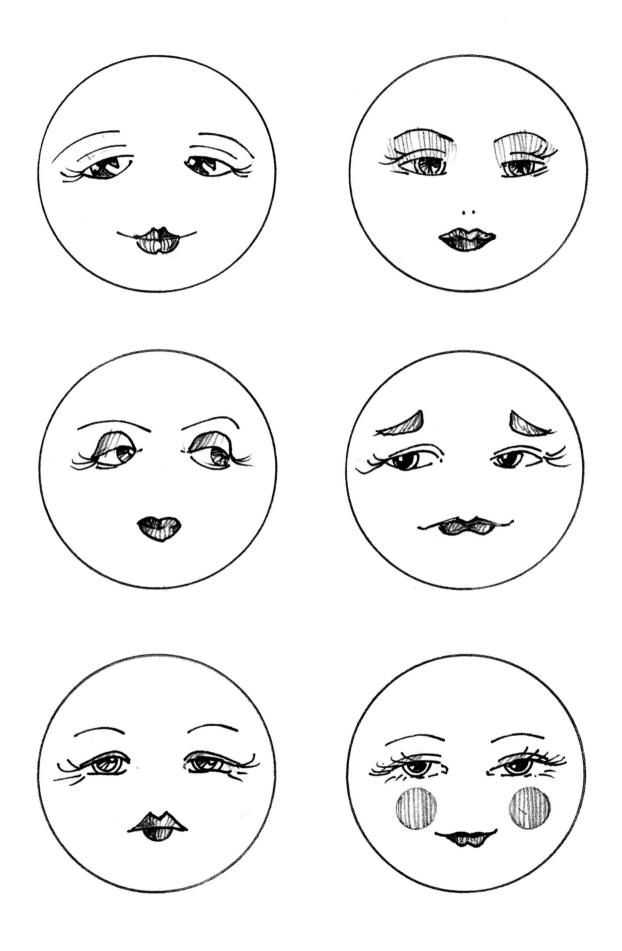

GENERAL INSTRUCTIONS

Cutting and Sewing

The patterns shown on pages 108 and 116 can be enlarged or reduced as you please. The pattern pieces as drawn include seam allowances; the sewing line is indicated as well because you will use this line in some of the methods described below. Remember as you sew that the printed black lines on any pattern can equal up to two widths of thread—almost a whole stitch—which means that you must sew consistently along the line. If you sew along the outside of the line, your doll will be ever so slightly larger. If you want to be very close to the sample, sew a few threads inside of the line you draw. When you use patterns that include the seam allowance, use your sewing machine foot as a guide to maintain a uniform seam allowance.

Durable Pattern Pieces

If you find a pattern you really like, it will be worth your time to make yourself a set of pattern pieces that will stand up to use and reuse. Trace or photocopy the pattern pieces onto plain paper, then use a glue stick to securely attach the paper pattern pieces to a piece of sturdy cardboard. Depending on the method you like to use, cut out the cardboard pieces along either the sewing line (eliminating any seam allowances) or the cutting line (including seam allowances). The cardboard will provide a firm edge when you trace, and it won't move around on your fabric or roll up at the edges as freezer paper and interfacing do.

To keep all the pieces together, punch a hole in each piece and string them together on a long string. For handy access, file the strings in a binder, along with the pattern envelope, photo, and instructions.

Standard Sewing

Make pattern pieces (see above), tracing the pattern along the cutting line. Place these pattern pieces on your fabric, trace around them, and cut the pieces out along the traced line. Yardages are based on 45" fabrics. When you sew the pieces together, be sure that you are using an accurate, consistent ¼" seam allowance, , unless indicated otherwise on the pattern pieces.

Transferring Face Designs

Ladies in the 1920s were just as hesitant about painting their dolls' faces as most of us are today. Their problem was easily solved because they could buy ready-made pressed cloth faces with printed features. While we are not so lucky, we have a far greater selection of fabric pens, fabric paints, and transfer techniques. Many of the cloth dolls made in the 1920s by such companies as Norah Wellings and Steiff had heads where basic long stitches from back to front to back suggested features, similar to today's soft-sculpture techniques.

Any face design can be traced onto fabric, and then embroidered or painted. The simplest way is to revert to a childhood trick: Use a pencil to trace darkly over the lines of the image, but on the *back* of the drawing. A lightbox or bright window is very helpful for this step. Lay the traced side on the fabric, and put pressure on the lines, or scribble with pencil just like you did in school, on top of the transfer design. A slightly higher-tech method to make patterns is to use tracing papers, which are available in fabric stores. If you're well-versed with your computer, purchase special printer-compatible iron-on transfer paper, scan the face design, print it out, and iron it on. Your local copy shop can also copy onto transfer paper for you.

APPLYING HAIR

Original applied hair was almost always wavy mohair or silk floss. You can usually find mohair curls on the doll supply shelf at your craft store, or order it via Internet sources. Look for silk floss in art needlework sources. If you're adding a hat, apply only enough hair to show around the edges.

Stitch or glue the hair to the head. For cloth heads, you can insert hair fiber with a felting needle for a nice effect, but this was not typical of the rapid "glue and go" manufactured types of earlier years. The felting needle is a long, thin, barbed piece of metal. Lay the hair fiber on the head and punch the needle into the head; this pushes the fiber into the head. After the head is covered, trim and style as you please. You can find sources for felting needles on page 127.

Page Sewing

I borrowed this term from Jane Wagner, who makes teeny-tiny felt dolls. I use this very efficient method for making dolls with identical parts, for instance, when the back and front pattern pieces are the same.

Make pattern pieces (see below), tracing the pattern along the sewing line, then cut out the pattern pieces along this line. Lay these pattern pieces on doubled fabric, folded and pinned in place with the right sides together, and trace around them to transfer the sewing line onto the fabric. Do not cut out the pieces. Sew along the drawn lines, leaving an opening for stuffing and turning. Cut out the sewn pieces, leaving a narrow seam allowance, between ⅛" and ¼". You'll find this method is faster, and you can trim seam allowances smaller, resulting in a less bulky seam line.

1. Make pattern pieces without the seam allowances.

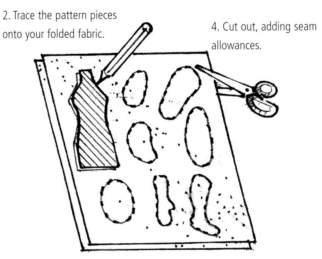

2. Trace the pattern pieces onto your folded fabric.

4. Cut out, adding seam allowances.

3. Sew along the drawn line, leaving opening for turning.

Page Sewing

Weight Bag

Even though most of these girls naturally flop and loll around, any bed-doll can benefit from a weight bag to help hold her in position. To make the bag, cut a piece of fabric, roughly in the shape shown below. Fold it in half and sew around the sides, leaving the bottom open. Look for BBs or fishing weights in sporting goods stores, and fill the bag with them (a funnel is helpful for pouring the BBs). Hand sew the weight bag closed. Stuff the torso, insert the weight bag in the lower torso, and hand sew with overcast stitches to close.

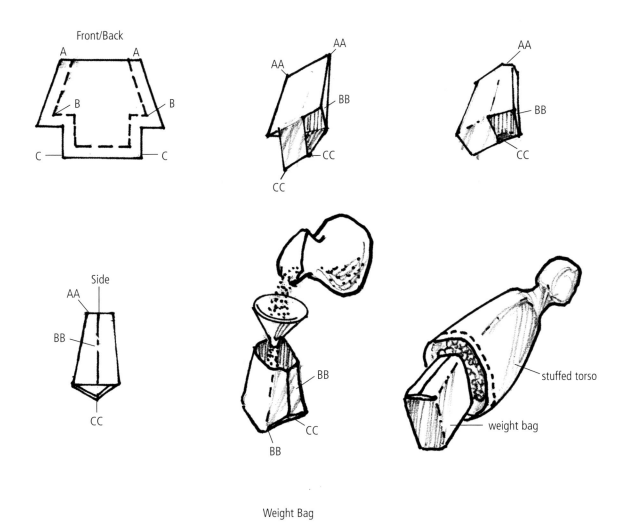

Weight Bag

Designer Gallery: New Dolls of the Era

So many people in the doll world are doll makers, not just doll collectors. Here are a few of their creations. Most of these were made to be reminiscent of Art Deco-era dolls; others (as you'll see) are just for fun. But all have their own personality, their own style, and their own flair.

Annabelle by Susanna Oroyan. This lovely doll is dressed in vintage fabrics.

Photos by W. Donald Smith

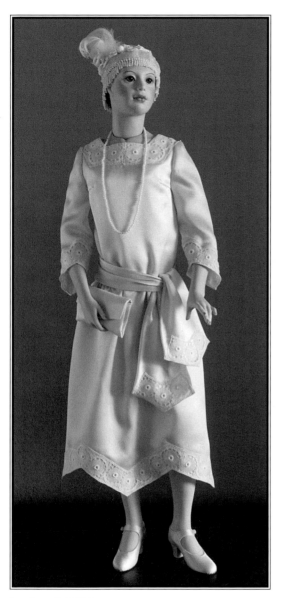

Lady of 1920 by Elisabeth Flueler-Tomamichel. This elegant flapper has a porcelain head on a wired armature body. Photo by Elisabeth Flueler-Tomamichel

Cheri by Charles Batte. This sculpted doll wears a vintage-styled costume. Photo by Jerry Anthony

Lady in Gray by Stella Emery. This lady was the very first doll Stella made. She was sculpted using Polyform clay. Photo by W. Donald Smith

Solange by Charles Batte. Like Cheri, Solange is dressed in exotic vintage style. Photo by Jerry Anthony

Gigi by Barbara Lady. This poor suffering soul is sculpted in Cernit.
Photo by W. Donald Smith

Elizabeth Brandon's porcelain picture of a jazz age lady putting on her make-up.
Photo by Berkley Brandon

Fan Dancer by Annie Wahl. This is a modern "vintage" piece—in more ways than one!
Photo by Tim Petros

Millie, a prototype made by the artist herself, shows Judi Ward's contemporary pattern for making a bed-doll in cloth.
Photo by W. Donald Smith

Rickety-Rackety Clown by Susanna Oroyan. Dip-Dot's cousin has a body and ruffles made of polished cotton—a print and a solid. Rickrack was a very popular trim of the era, as was the Harlequin theme, so I combined them to create this doll. The back of his head is black (to suggest a clown's skullcap). His simple cone-shape hat is made from printed fabric with a felt brim. His hair is glued-on fringe.
Photo by W. Donald Smith

Homage to Erté by Christine Shively. This doll shows what a difference detailed face painting can make to the Basic Bobbie pattern. Her elaborate costuming includes metallic velvet crinkle fabric, seed beads, manipulated fabric, and a gold crinkle plume on her hat. Photo by W. Donald Smith

Josephine by Patti LaValley. This variation of the Basic Bobbie pattern has a needle-sculpted head covered with Creative Paperclay to give it a hard, paintable surface. Patti redrew the hand portion of the pattern so that Josephine could hold a cigarette between her separate fingers. She is costumed in vintage fabrics. Photo by W. Donald Smith

Tropical Entertainer by Susanna Oroyan. Hawaii and the Caribbean were just getting to be known as tourist destinations in the flapper era. Tourists—who had to take the boat—often liked to bring back souvenir dolls that represented the people and the local entertainment they had seen. This doll's body is made of bronze-colored velour; 1920s versions were made in heavier velveteen. The stitched-on hair is black polyester stuffing; great when you're using a darker-color fabric for the body. Costume ideas for her could include a lei of gathered rickrack; a grass skirt of raffia, fringe, or felt; a flowered tropical print fabric for the torso; and a straw hat—look in the doll accessories section at your local craft store. Photo by W. Donald Smith

A delightful all-original pincushion just 4" tall. This doll was obviously well-used—I found hundreds of pins and needles in the old base. Photo by W. Donald Smith

A fabulous 1920's purse—yes it's a real one—with flapper head and legs. Photo by W. Donald Smith

Cloth mask-face jewelry or lingerie bag with peach velvet and pearls. Photo by Maralyn Christoffersen

A cloth mask doll head mounted on a pale green taffeta pillow with a ruffled cap to match. Photo by W. Donald Smith

This painted composition doll has a wide base. I had purchased the legs several years ago. When a friend asked me to fix this doll, I discovered the legs were the same material and matched wonderfully. Photo by W. Donald Smith

Basic Bobbie

This very basic pattern is an easy way for any doll maker to put her toe in the water. The chunky feet and plain, rectangular body are really very like the body construction of many of the older dolls. Homemade dolls of the Art Deco era often were pieced together with whatever was on hand; you can mimic this look by using a combination of printed and textured fabrics for the body parts. An added benefit is that you don't have to make an additional costume right away—the doll is its own costume. Pick and choose from the faces on pages 92 and 93, then paint or embroider as desired.

Dip-Dot Clown by Susanna Oroyan. This basic stuffed fabric doll is easily made into a clever character. Dip-Dot has glued-on embroidery floss hair, and his folded-newspaper hat is made of organdy. His gathered tulle neck ruffle and the ruffles at his wrists and ankles pull the clown "costume" together.
Photo by W. Donald Smith

Materials and Supplies

You will need a total of about one yard of fabric. Specific yardage is not given so you can mix and match scraps. Options include polished cotton, medium-weight muslin, or lightweight oilcloth. Alternatively, try painting the whole body with flesh-colored acrylic paint. Paint the facial features, and then give the whole doll a coat of gloss acrylic.

Construction

Enlarge the pattern pieces and make pattern pieces for the head, body, arms, and legs. There are two head options. The first is what I call a double pillow: two round "pillows" sewn together to make a fuller head shape. The second is a two-piece head: one pillow stitched to a stuffed head back that looks sort of like a hood and helps to avoid "neck flop" when the stuffing sags. Sew the head back pieces together, leaving the bottom open. Stuff and sew to the pillow. Extend the flaps of the head backs on either side of the neck and sew them to the neck.

The shape and construction of this doll also give you a lot of different possibilities beyond the clown doll. Check the photos that follow to see what other doll makers have done with this pattern. The body pattern is generic enough that you can use it with the arms, legs, and head patterns here, or with your own original sculpted parts. If you'd like, add some simple needle-sculptured features. I like to add decorative details, like the shoe detail that I borrowed from one of my vintage dolls. I have also marked the body pattern so you can use it to replace a body on an old commercial flange or shoulder head.

To assemble the doll, sew and stuff the arms, legs, body, and head. Gather the openings, and stitch the body parts onto the body with hidden stitches.

Pattern Pieces for Basic Bobbie

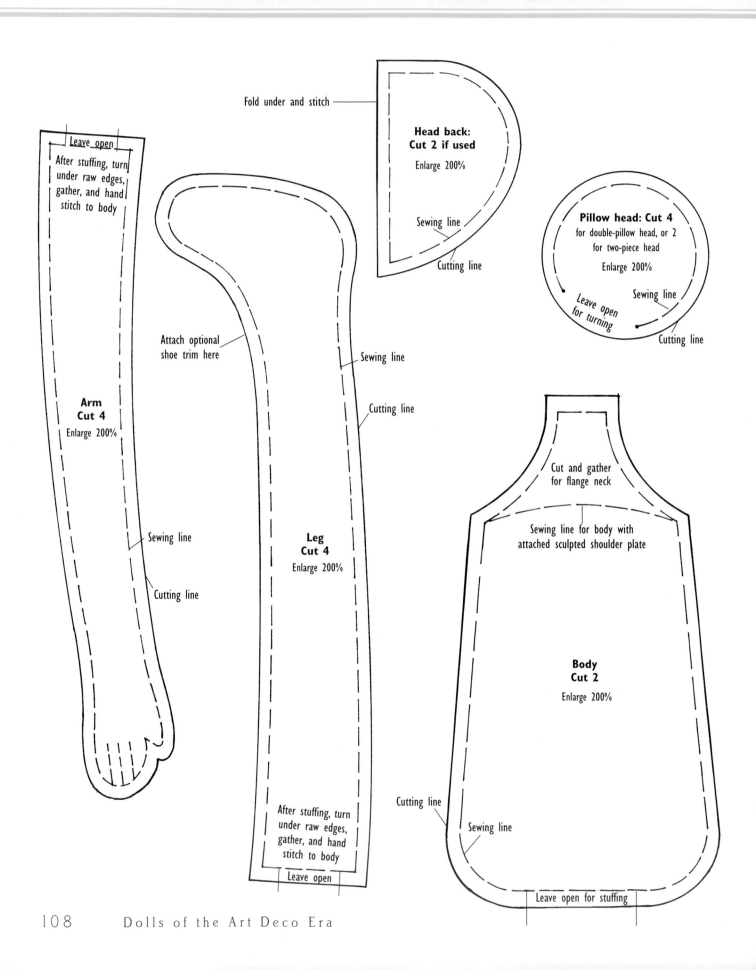

Fold under and stitch

**Head back:
Cut 2 if used**

Enlarge 200%

Sewing line

Cutting line

Pillow head: Cut 4
for double-pillow head, or 2
for two-piece head

Enlarge 200%

Sewing line

Leave open
for turning

Cutting line

Leave open

After stuffing, turn
under raw edges,
gather, and hand
stitch to body

Attach optional
shoe trim here

Sewing line

Cutting line

**Arm
Cut 4**

Enlarge 200%

Sewing line

Cutting line

Cut and gather
for flange neck

Sewing line for body with
attached sculpted shoulder plate

**Leg
Cut 4**

Enlarge 200%

**Body
Cut 2**

Enlarge 200%

Cutting line

Sewing line

After stuffing, turn
under raw edges,
gather, and hand
stitch to body

Leave open

Leave open for stuffing

Head Option I
Double-Pillow Head

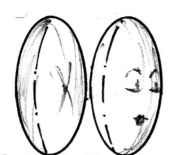
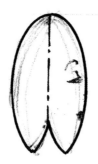

1. Double pillow head

2. Stitch head backs together

Head Option II
Two-Piece Head

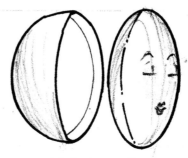
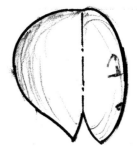

1. Stuff and sew to pillow

2. Attach two-piece head to neck

Basic Bobbie's Hat

Hat

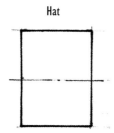

1. Fold in half

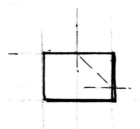

2. Fold down corners

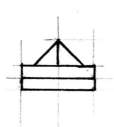

3. Fold up bottom edges

4. Tack corners to hold

1. Foot with instep curve and ruffle

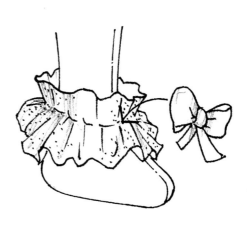

2. Optional: sew separate shoe of silk; slip over foot; trim with lace and ribbon

Betty, The Bee's Knees

Simple cloth dolls with arms tied over folded knees—often not dressed—commonly sat on college dormitory dressing tables. In their day, they would have been termed "decorators." Smoking, then considered a liberated, thoroughly modern, supposedly healthful thing to do, was a popular theme in the boudoir doll genre.

When she dressed, Betty wore typical lounging garb of the era: teddy lingerie and a kimono. If you don't want to make this doll a costume, consider making her body from printed fabric. Velveteen would make her quite swanky.

This project gives you the opportunity to try simple sculpture. In the early days, Betty would be made with either a cloth head or a purchased molded composition head. If you want to exercise the smoking option, you will need to model the head—just a basic egg with some slight embellishments. Refer to the photos as you go along.

Betty the Bee's Knees by Susanna Oroyan. Betty isn't anywhere near the bad girl she would like you to think she is. With her deliberate pose and languid eyelids, this "hep" college coed is affecting the look of the sultry siren, *femme fatale* heroine of the silver screen. She just knows that if she gets that look right, there is a Rudolph Valentino-type who will come to sweep her off her feet. Photo by W. Donald Smith

Modeling the Head

You will need:

❖ 1 foot of kitchen aluminum foil
❖ 8-ounce package of Creative Paperclay
❖ Water spray bottle
❖ Metal fingernail file, orange stick, or sculpture tools

1. Crumple the foil to make a rough egg shape 2½" tall. Flatten pieces of the Paperclay to about ¼" thick, and press onto your egg shape—a real egg helps for comparison. The Paperclay will stabilize as you build; be patient, and use the spray bottle to keep the surface smooth and blended as you work Use the metal file to smooth the surface; fingertips tend to create bumps. When you finish, your egg should be about 3" tall. Hold it up and draw a light line down the center to check that the halves are symmetrical.

Cover the foil with Paperclay   Smooth the surface into an egg shape

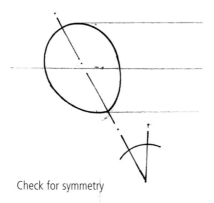

Check for symmetry

2. Hold the egg with the pointy end down. Look straight at the egg, and use the fingernail file to mark light lines to divide the face horizontally, as shown, into rough thirds. Hold the egg in both hands and use your thumbs to make slight depressions at about the halfway point of the head. These shallow hollows will be Betty's eye sockets. You'll hold the head at a slight angle, as shown, to complete her facial features.

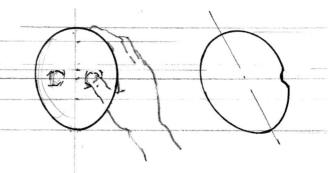

A. Indentations form eye sockets   B. Hold the head at an angle

3. Make a ⅝"-diameter ball of Paperclay; position it as shown for the nose. Blend the ball into a slightly triangular "mountain ridge" shape, then add a smaller ball to each side, as shown. Blend into a smooth nose shape. Make a slight indent above the nose between the eyes.

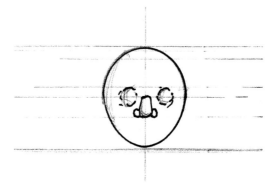

Add the nose, keeping it moist as you sculpt it

4. Add a small piece of Paperclay to the face just below the nose to form the upper lip/mouth. Press lightly to indent the lower lip area. The head should resemble the profile in the illustration.

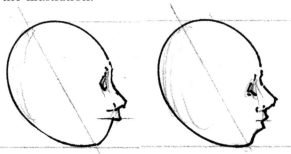

Add a small ball underneath the nose and sculpt it into the upper lip

Form the lower lip and chin with a small depression

5. Form the lip line by making a shallow cut with edge of the file. Use the drawing below as a reference for the width and depth of the cut. Insert the file between the lips, and exert very gentle pressure as you rock it up and down to open up the lips. Use the point of the tool to press in lightly at each corner of the mouth.

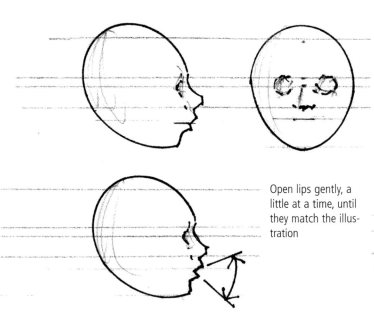

Open lips gently, a little at a time, until they match the illustration

6. To give her lips that pouty fullness, make three small balls of Paperclay, and apply them to the lips as shown: two to the underside of the upper lip, and one on the lower lip. Smooth the edges to form a Cupid's bow shape.

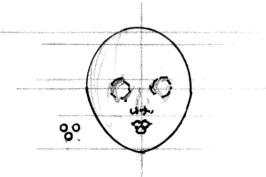

Press the balls onto the lips to make them full

7. Add a thin ¾"-diameter pancake of Paperclay to the top half of the eye indent. Smooth to form the lid, and use the file to score the lid line, as shown. If you would like a droopy-lidded, half-closed eye, stop here. To make an open eye, add a tiny ball of clay below the lash line, and flatten it slightly. Remember, you wouldn't see the full, round eyeball unless she was surprised or scared. Cut away the clay at the top and bottom of the eye, using the illustrations for reference.

Tip: Check your work in front of a mirror. The image in the mirror should appear the same as the real head—symmetrical, not lopsided.

8. Carefully remove a small part of the clay from the sides of the head to create the temple depressions above the sides of the eyes. Cut away a 1½"-diameter circle at the center bottom to make a hole for the fabric neck. Use a toothpick to make a hole in the mouth for the cigarette. When you are satisfied with the head, use a soft, wet paintbrush to smooth the surface.

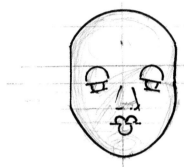

Slice a little at a time to form the temples, and cut away the clay at the bottom.

9. Set the head aside to air-dry for three days. Or, speed up the process by putting the head in a 150° oven, leaving the door open. The head will be dry in eight to ten hours. Clay dries from the outside in, forming a crust that can crack, particularly at the neck opening. If it does, don't despair. Make a paste of dampened Paperclay, wet the cracked edges, and fill in any open spaces. After the head has dried, it should feel lighter in your hand and appear white. Use a pair of needlenose pliers to reach into the hole from the bottom. Gently grasp and twist the foil until it compresses within the head. Pull the foil out, in pieces if necessary, through the neck opening. The head will be hollow, but

it might still be damp inside and very fragile. Do not continue until the clay is thoroughly dry inside and out.

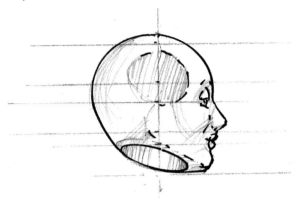

Use pliers to remove the foil from inside the head

10. When the clay is completely dry, sand the head lightly and gently with fine sandpaper. If you need to fill in areas, use a spray water bottle to dampen the surface, then stick dampened Paperclay to the surface. When you are satisfied, go over sanded head with a wet paintbrush, and let the head dry completely.

11. Paint the head with acrylic flesh-tone paint. Thin the paint with water and apply three to five light layers. When dry, use a light pencil to sketch the facial features onto the head. Paint the features with acrylic paint in this order:

❖ White of the eye

❖ Eye color; use a toothpick to add a dot of black paint for pupil and a dot of white paint for highlight

❖ Black lash line and eyebrow (or use a nib pen with brown ink)

❖ Red mouth

❖ Pink cheeks

12. Finish the head with a coat of spray acrylic sealer. Choose either a matte or gloss finish as you please.

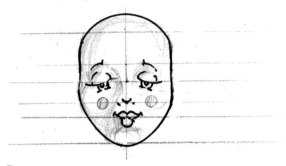

Tip: If you have trouble controlling a paintbrush, use a toothpick to dab paint on, since these features are very simple dots. If you have trouble painting eyes/brows on the same line, turn the head upside down to paint the second one. This will put your good hand on the difficult side.

Body Assembly

You will need:

❖ **¾ yard cotton, velvet, or polished cotton fabric**

Enlarge the patterns and make pattern pieces for the body, arms, and legs. Cut, sew, turn, and stuff the pieces as directed on the patterns. Use a ¼" seam when sewing. If desired, add a weight bag to the bottom of the body to stabilize Betty in a sitting position, or sew her to a pillow later. Turn under the raw edges of the arms, gather, and stitch the arms to the body. The Basic Betty sits with her knees up under her chin. Pin the legs to the body and test their length, shortening them if necessary. Turn under the raw edges at the top of the legs and stitch them to the body. Tie the arms around the folded legs, as shown in the photograph on page 110.

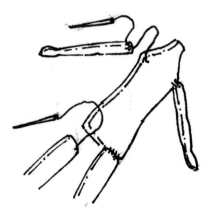

Hand sew the arms and legs to the body

To attach the head, run a line of glue around the cloth neck top. Place the head over the neck stub, and set in place.

If you would like the head to move, drill a hole in the top of the head. Before stuffing the body, sew a 4-hole button to the inside of the neck top, using only two of the holes to sew it on. Run a 12" length of 16-gauge wire through the remaining holes in the button so that two wires, each approximately 6" long, stick out of the neck top. Place the head over the neck top so the wires extend through the hole in top of the head. Push the neck well into head, and run the wires through another button on top of the head opening. Twist the wires together, then trim and flatten them close to the head.

Betty's Costume

Teddy: Wrap a length of 3"-wide lace around the body, trim, turn under ends at center back, and hand sew seam to join. Tack lace between legs at crotch with thread or a short strip of ¼" lace. Add shoulder straps made of ⅛"-wide silk ribbon. Trim or embellish with silk ribbon bows or roses.

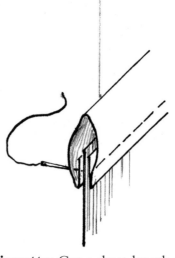

Fold ribbon in half, turn under edges, and sew to raw edge of kimono

Kimono: You will need an 18" x 25" rectangle of sheer fabric.

Enlarge pattern. Fold fabric once in half, and then in half again, so there are four thicknesses of fabric. Place pattern piece so top of sleeve is at the double folds and front/back line is on the single fold. Cut out kimono. Cut center front and trim neckline as shown. Fold kimono right sides together, match As and Bs and sew the front and back together from the bottom of each sleeve (A) down the side seam to the bottom (B). Turn under the raw edges at the sleeve ends and bottom edge, and hand sew a narrow hem. Sew ⅝"-wide ribbon around the neck opening, to form a bound edge. Add a ribbon tie belt, if desired.

Cigarette: Cut a short length of ³⁄₁₆"-diameter dowel, wooden skewer, or round toothpick. Paint the cigarette white, and then dip the "burning" end in red paint.

Hair: Cut a 6" length of wefted curly mohair. Roll the banded edge into a circle, and stitch to secure. Spread the hair away from the center, apply glue under the center, and stick the hair to the head. Keep the hair loose for flyaway hair, or glue it down for a more controlled hairstyle.

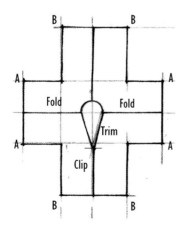

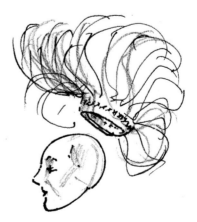

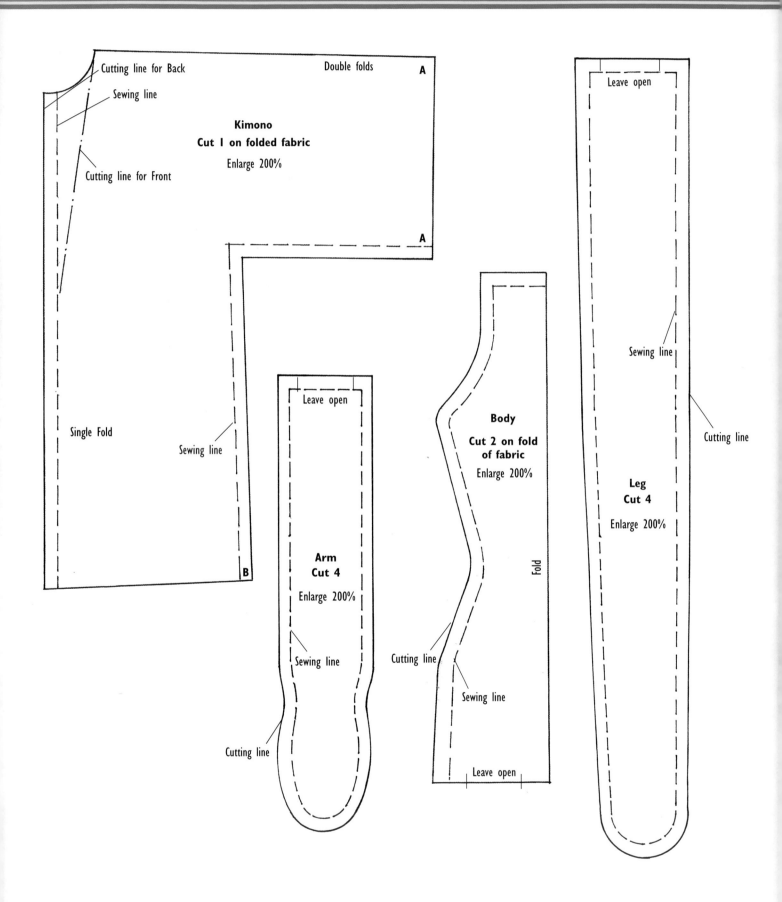

Cutting line for Back

Sewing line

Double folds

A

Kimono
Cut 1 on folded fabric
Enlarge 200%

Cutting line for Front

A

Single Fold

Sewing line

B

Leave open

Arm
Cut 4

Enlarge 200%

Sewing line

Cutting line

Leave open

Body
Cut 2 on fold of fabric

Enlarge 200%

Cutting line

Sewing line

Fold

Leave open

Leave open

Sewing line

Cutting line

Leg
Cut 4

Enlarge 200%

Betty's Friends

Artist Inez Brasch took one look at a photo of Betty and came up with three different sculpted heads for a girl of her ilk. Here, we are trying them on the typical posed body to see which one we like best. Photo by W. Donald Smith

Mahjong Madness by Susanna Oroyan. This version of Betty has sculpted arms and legs that can easily be used with the body pattern given here. Take a look at her accessories, too—this lounger has the typical kimono, a couple of pillows for comfort, a typically long string of beads, and, of course, her mahjong set. Photo W. Donald Smith

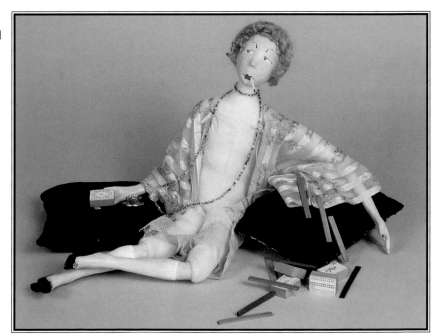

Accessories for Your Dolls

Once you start making your own dolls, you'll certainly need to provide them with all their basic needs—companions, comfort, and trappings. Magazines and craft books of the era showed dolls on pillows, surrounded by feather or net ruffles. Use your imagination and take a look at the accessories the dolls in this book have, and you'll find there's no end to the knick-knacks you can whip up for your girls.

These shadow boxes have plenty of ideas for accessories for your dolls. *Right:* silk sachets, flapper face pin, garter, silk ribbon flowers, painted composition bust with original metal hands and a tiny nodder doll. *Above:* cloth mask face from a purchased kit, silk sachets, garter, typical bed-doll hands, and a tiny doll purse with a bag formed with a mirror.
Photos by W. Donald Smith

Bed-Doll Dogs

If your dolls seem lonely, they might need a decorator doggie. This pattern is for a generic breed so you can decide about long or short legs, tail, and hair. Do note that this is meant to be a hairy dog, covered with fur or fiber. If you haven't been to a yarn shop lately, do go, and have fun selecting some wonderful fibers to create this pet and to use as embellishment for your other doll projects. Don't forget dogs wear things, too! Add a hat and coat, or a fancy jeweled collar.

Choo-Choo de Pooch and **Della O'Dawg** by Susanna Oroyan. Classy, long-haired Choo-Choo *(right)* has fur made by combining variegated knitting ribbon with two decorator yarns, which are looped and stitched along the dog's back, tail, and chest. Knotted loops stitched to the head form the ears and tail. Della *(left)* is made from the same pattern; the tips of her legs bend to form paws. Her fur is made of two layered decorator yarns. Photo by W. Donald Smith

You need:

- ¼ yard felt, velour, velvet or woolen fabric
- Felt scraps
- Metal coat hanger or 4' of 16-gauge wire
- Your choice of fibers to finish hair:
  For longhaired dog, use mohair yarn
  For poodle, finish with pom-poms
  For short curly hair, use sheepskin or similar fleece fabric

1. Sew and turn body.

2. Sew and turn legs. Insert wire in legs, Stuff. Make X-shaped cut on each side of body and push legs through. Bend as shown to make dog stand. To position or close hole, stitch legs to body where they come through opening. Use a pair of needle-nose pliers to bend legs to make paws, if desired.

3. Stuff dog body. Sew opening closed. Make tail. Poke hole and insert. Secure with stitches.

4. Sew ½" dome shaped button for nose. Sew ⅜" flat buttons for eyes and nose. If preferred, cut eyes out of felt and glue on head. Embroider nose.

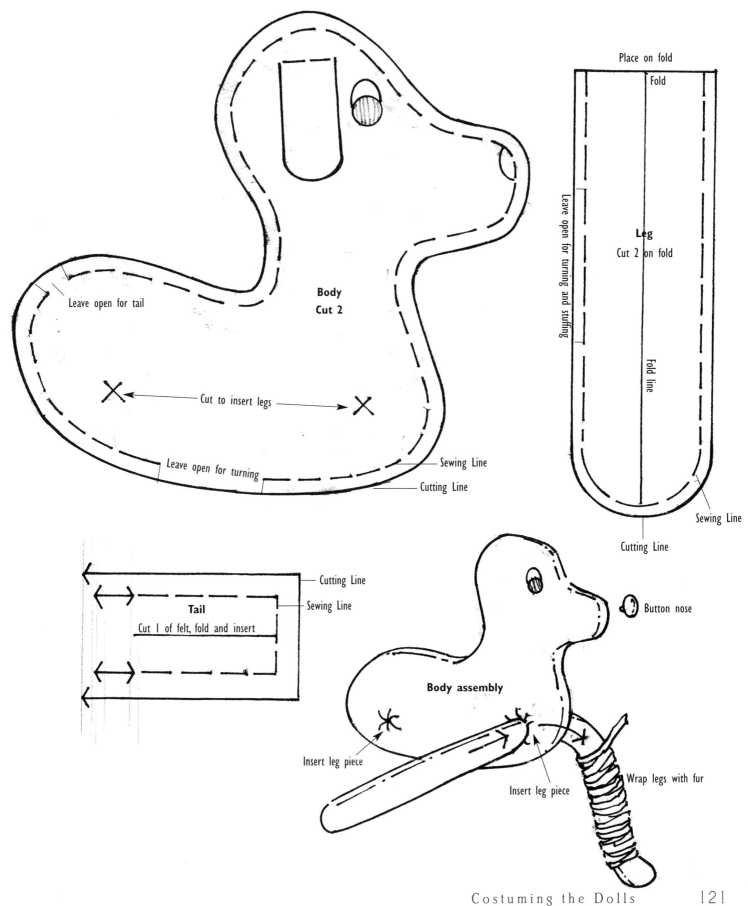

Leave open for tail

Body
Cut 2

✕ ⟵ Cut to insert legs ⟶ ✕

Leave open for turning

Sewing Line

Cutting Line

Place on fold

Fold

Leave open for turning and stuffing

Leg
Cut 2 on fold

Fold line

Sewing Line

Cutting Line

Cutting Line

Sewing Line

Tail
Cut 1 of felt, fold and insert

Button nose

Body assembly

Insert leg piece

Insert leg piece

Wrap legs with fur

A Passel of Pooches

Right and center: *Mac* and *Toby* by Jean Peeters. These pups, a terrier and an Australian shepherd, have needle-felted coats, button eyes and nose, and lots of charm. Mac sports a tartan plaid coat, and Toby's collar even has an ID tag. Dog on left, by Saralee Hesse, was made with multicolored specialty fabrics. Photo by W. Donald Smith

Left: *Pegadog* by Leilani Lyons. His shiny blue coat is made of thick fibers, and he's beaded to make him extra-fancy. Right: *Charlie* by Susan Colvin. This black poodle is bursting with energy and fun; see his poodle topknot?
Photo by W. Donald Smith

Bed dolls love their pets. Here, a lovely silk mask-face doll displays her appliquéd organdy skirt sitting on a park bench with her adorable pooch.
Photo by W. Donald Smith

Tassel Dolls

Tassel Dolls by Susanna
Oroyan. These little dolls are just
plain fun—and totally accessible for
any age doll maker. Use your imagination and your scraps to see what
you can come up with.
Photo by W. Donald Smith

In the Art Deco era, dolls appeared not only as dolls; they also showed
up decorating—or as integral parts of—hundreds of accessories. These
little "charm"ers might have dangled from handbags, fans, pincushions,
car windows, lamp bases, shade pulls, curtain tassels, tie backs…well,
you get the idea. They're so quick and fun to whip up; you'll find yourself with tassel dolls all over your house!

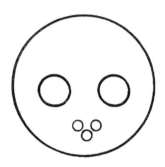

Materials and Supplies

❖ Assorted wooden and painted beads (large wooden macramé beads can be found at craft suppliers)

❖ Assorted drapery tassels (check your local fabric store or upholstery supplier)

❖ Heavy cord and/or thread

❖ Paints or markers

Tip: If you would like to try this from the ground up, use fringes to make a tassel. Design a torso and sew it to the top of your tassel.

Use these examples for ideas when you paint the bead heads for your tassel dolls.

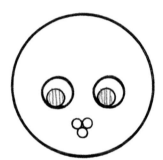
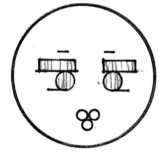
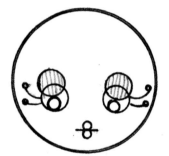
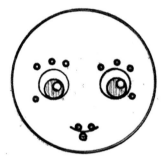

Once you have painted the wooden bead heads and let them dry, you can use your imagination to come up with any type of body you'd like! Photo by W. Donald Smith

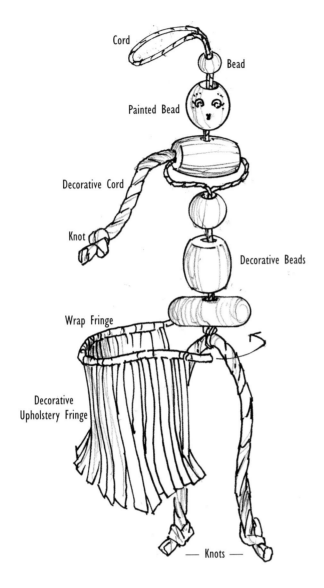

Cord

Bead

Painted Bead

Decorative Cord

Knot

Decorative Beads

Wrap Fringe

Decorative
Upholstery Fringe

— Knots —

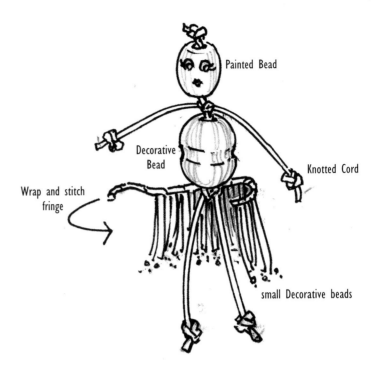

Painted Bead

Decorative
Bead

Wrap and stitch
fringe

Knotted Cord

small Decorative beads

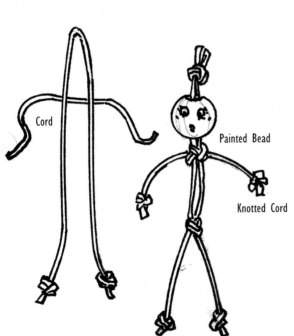

Cord

Painted Bead

Knotted Cord

Gail Lackey went a little farther with this tassel doll—she has a sculpted head and molded hands. She is quite elegant and is typical of more modern-day tassel designs. Photo by Gail Lackey

About the Author and the Artists

Susanna Oroyan taught herself the art of dollmaking. She has made and collected dolls actively since 1972, and her dollmaking has become a full-time career. For the past decade Susanna has been a motivating force in regional and national dollmaker organizations. She has exhibited her dolls internationally, and in 1995 she received the Dollmaker of the Year Award at the National Cloth Doll Festival. Susanna is the author of *Fantastic Figures, Anatomy of the Doll, Designing the Doll,* and *Finishing the Figure* and has written numerous articles for doll magazines. She has also taught dollmaking classes at many major conferences as well as for dollmaking groups. Susanna's cloth doll patterns are available from:

Fabricat Design • 3270 Whitbeck Boulevard • Eugene, OR 97405

The Artists

Again, my thanks to the artists who took time to create samples of the pattern projects and share photos of their work. Those listed below teach classes, have instructional materials and patterns, or create original dolls for collectors. If you contact any by mail, please enclose a self-addressed, stamped envelope for a prompt reply.

Brasch, Inez, 210 Rustic Place, Columbia, OH 43214
Culea, Patti, 9019 Stargaze Venue, San Diego, CA 92119
Esslinger, Drusilla, R#2 Box 630, Madison, KS 66860
Groves, Bonnie, 402 North Avenue A, Elgin, TX 78621
Lady, Barbara, 1036 Easy Street, Brookings, OR 97415
LaValley, Patti, 30065 Northrup Road NW, North Plains, OR 97133
McCullough, Julie, 439 Chestnut Street, Lancaster, PA 17603
Robertson, Virginia, P.O. Box 357, Dolores, CO 81323
Shively, Christine, 8717 Hilltop Road, Ozwakie, KS 66070
Ward, Judi, P.O. Box 1015, St. Helens, OR 97051

Charles Batte, Stephanie Blythe, Elizabeth Brandon, Elisabeth Fleuler-Tomomicheal, Gail Lackey, and Annie Wahl may be contacted through the National Institute of American Doll Artists at www.NIADA.org.

Sources

Farago, Stephanie. 1986. *The Magic and Romance of Art-dolls.* Farago Publications, P.O. Box 48200, Los Angeles, CA 90048.

Brill, Patricia. "American Boudoir Dolls," *Dolls,* September 2002 and December 2002.

Christoffersen, Maralyn, and Estelle Johnston. "Beautiful Boudoir Dolls," *Doll Reader,* May 1994.

Christoffersen, Maralyn, and Estelle Johnston. "Boudoir Dolls of Cloth," *Doll Reader,* July 1994 and September 1994.

Christoffersen, Maralyn, and Estelle Johnston. "Boudoir Smokers," *Doll Reader,* August 1995.

Groves, Bonnie. "Lenci Fadettes: Inspiration for Cubeb Type Smokers?" *Antique Doll Collector,* November 2002.

Groves, Bonnie. "Stunning Sterling Boudoir Dolls," *Antique Doll Collector,* January 2002.

Also see your library for books containing the works of fashion designers and illustrators of the era: *Erté, Poiret,* and *Barbier,* and for doll collector magazines.

Air-drying/oven-curing clays

Creative Paperclay
Company, Inc.
79 Daily Drive, Suite 101
Camarillo, CA 93010
www.paperclay.com

Handcraft Designs
63 East Broad Street
Hatfield, PA 19940
www.hdclays.com

Sculpey
Polyform Products
1901 Estes Avenue
Elk Grove, IL 60007
www.sculpey.com

Dollmaking supplies

Virginia Robertson
Hard-to-Find Catalog
P.O. Box 357
Dolores, CO 81323

Sisters and Daughters
465 North Burkhart Road
Howell, MI 48843
(800) 250-507
www.clothdoll.com

Fancy Fabrics and Embellishments

Pamela Armas
Treasures of the Gypsy
P.O. Box 748
Mountainair, NM 87036
(505) 847-0963

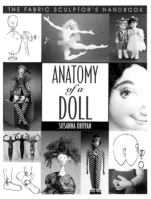

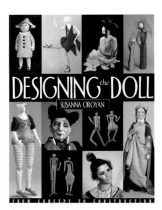

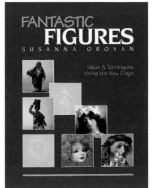

Index

Accessories, 118

Acrylic paints, 68

All original (AO), defined, 44

Alma Company, 60

Altbuck, H., 37

American Stuffed Novelty Company, 51

Anita Novelty Company, 37, 52–53

Anita–type dolls, 4, 9, 28, 30, 34, 41, 42, 44, 49

Art Deco style, 15, 23, 88–89, 91

Art dolls, 15, 18, 23, 25, 64

Art Nouveau, 23

Auctions, 43

Bed dolls, 7, 8–13, 15, 17, 18, 19, 30, 34, 35, 40–43, 47, 64–65, 69, 75

Black Bottom dolls, 37, 38

Bleach, 66

Bloom dolls, 37, 48

Blossom–type dolls, 5, 24, 37, 42, 43, 44, 63, 83

Bobbie doll, pattern, 106–109

Body fabric for making dolls, 89

Boudoir dolls, 17, 18, 19

Brasch, Inez, 117

Brazilian dolls, 38, 58

Breastplate, 45

Buster Brown dolls, 35

Button joints, 45

Café Society dolls, 63

Celluclay II, 68

Chad Valley Toy Company, 15, 37, 39

Cleaning doll bodies, 66–67

Cloth bodies, rebuilding, 68

Cloth or stuffed cloth, 45, 64, 66–67

Clown dolls, 15, 28, 32, 37, 60, 62

C&O Dressel flapper doll, 31

Collecting dolls, 34–39, 40–43

Colors, choosing for doll construction, 92

Columbine, 60

Commédia style, 18, 38, 60–61

Common dolls, 36

Composition dolls, 45, 64, 67

Composition and cloth dolls, 36

Costume fabric, 89

Costuming dolls, 90–91

Cracks, repairing, 67

Crazing, 45

Creative Paperclay, 68

Cubeb smoker dolls, 26, 34, 35, 38, 42, 79, 82

Dancing dolls, 37

Dean's, 15

Dogs, bed–doll, 119–21

Doll dress patterns, McCall's, 27

Doll fad, post World War I, 23

Doll parts, rebuilding, 68

Dolls made between 1920–1940, mid–1930s–1940s, characteristics of, 47

Erasing soil, 65–66

Erté, 15

Etta–type dolls, 5, 28, 37, 49, 51

European Doll Manufacturing Company, 37

Face designs, 92–93, 95

Facial features, characteristics, 48–53

Farrago, Stephanie, 91

Flange head, 45

Flapper dolls, 17, 18–19, 24, 31, 78, 81, 104

French Dollmakers, Gre Poir, 37

French dolls, 18, 25, 29, 37, 44, 56–57

Gerling Company, 38, 49, 50

German–made dolls, 25, 45

Grazing, 45

Hair, 69, 95

Half–dolls, 74

Harlequin dolls, 18, 60

Harper's Bazaar, 15

Hats, 89

Hat stands, 61

Holzer et cie, 38

Inset, 45

Internet, buying dolls on, 40, 43

Italian souvenir doll, 57

Jane Gray Company, 38, 50

Jewelry bag doll, 105

Keeneye, 35, 39

Keney, Victor, 39

Kidd, Etta, 37

Kits, 47

Kuddle dolls, 38, 50

Lafitte Desirat, 15, 38

Laundering, 66

Lenci Company, and dolls, 15, 19, 36, 38, 42, 59, 80, 81, 89

Les Poupee's Gerb's, 15, 38, 50, 56

Lillie Baitz, 14, 47

Madame Marter, 14

The Magic and Romance of Art Dolls, 91

Manufacturer's marks, 35

Marie Antoinette style, 18, 54, 56

Marked dolls, defined, 44

Mascot dolls, 17, 18

Mascottes, by Lenci, 38

Mask face, 45, 68

Melting, 45

Metal joints, 45

Mint or Mint–in–box, defined, 44

Mohair, 69

Molded face, 45

Molded on, 46

Movies, development of and dolls, 16–17

Musee des Arts Decoratifs, 38

Mutual Novelty Company, 38

Naroditskya, Irma, 16

1920s, influence of on dolls, 15–17, 18, 20–22, 23

Norah Wellings company, 19, 33, 95

Novelty dolls, 10, 19

Page sewing, 96

Pajama bags, 15

Paper towel, for pattern pieces, 89

Patterns, 94

Paul Poiret, 15

Perk!, for stain removal, 66

Poir, Eugene, 37

Pierette style, 18, 60, 61, 62

Pierrot style, 18, 60, 61, 62

Pillow dolls, 18

Pincushion doll, 25, 104

Pin joints, 46

Pressed face or head, 45

Prices of dolls, 41–43

Purse doll, flapper, 104

Repairs, types of, 64–69, 70–77

Restoration, 64–65

Restored or repaired, defined, 44

Rubs, 46

Rust, paste formula for removal of, 66

Scaveni, Elena, 38

Schelhorn Company, 62

Sewing dolls, 94, 96

Shattering, 45

Shoes, 89

Sleep–eye, 46

Smoker dolls, 18, 26, 31, 62, 63, 78–83, 84, 88

Sofa dolls, 18

Spanish style, 58–59

Specialty fabrics, techniques for, 66

Stain removal, 66

Standard Doll Company, 39

Steiff, 19, 95

Sterling dolls, 32, 39

Storage, 69

Stuffing, 46

Swivel head, 45

Tagged, defined, 44

Tassel dolls, 122–24

Turn–head, 45, 52

Unique Novelty Doll Company, 28, 39

Vacuuming, 65

Vamp style, 19

Victorian era, 23

Vintage, defined, 44

Wagner, Jane, 96

Wax–covered composition dolls, 33

Weight bags, 97

Wellings, Norah, 39

Whitening, 66

Whoopee dolls, 37

Wigs, 66, 69

W–K–S.–type dolls, 5, 18, 26, 35

Wobblies, 18

World I, and European art–doll movement, 14–15, 16–17

Wright's Silver Polish, 67

Zaga of Zona, 76–77